The Dog Scrap Book

Bull Terrier Edition

Vintage Dog Books
Home Farm
44 Evesham Road
Cookhill, Alcester
Warwickshire
B49 5LJ

www.vintagedogbooks.com

ISBN No. 978-1-84664-846-5

Published by Vintage Dog Books 2006
Vintage Dog Books is an imprint of Read Books

British Library Cataloguing-in-Publication Data
A catalogue record for this book is available
from the British Library.

Vintage Dog Books
Home Farm
44 Evesham Road
Cookhill, Alcester
Warwickshire
B49 5LJ

If you and ourselves were as good humans as dogs are good dogs, if you and ourselves lived up to the opportunities and possibilities the Creator has given us as well as the dog does to his, most of us would be farther on the way to heaven and eternal glory than we actually are.

DON'T CALL A MAN A DOG

WHEN we consider how loyal the dog is, even to an evil, cruel master . . . .

WHEN we consider how patient the dog is in this hurly-burly world of ours . . . .

WHEN we consider how the dog possesses the cardinal virtue we humans lack most—to forgive fully . . . .

WHEN we consider how the dog enters wholeheartedly into whatever task is assigned him, unpleasant tho it may be . . . .

WHEN we consider that man is the most selfish, designing creature on earth and his dog the most unselfish living thing in the world, risking even life without hesitation . . . .

WHEN we consider how the dog lives a wholesome filosofy of enjoying every passing moment, finding daily delite in living, and to his dying day, retaining a heart of youth . . . .

WHEN we consider how, in the home, the dog by practice and self-example, is a teacher to children and grownups of such qualities as responsibility, obedience, kindness and social altruism . . . .

WHEN we consider all these things and that the dog is the nearest approach on earth to the actual living of the teachings of Jesus of Nazareth . . . .

WHEN we consider all these things —

DON'T CALL A MAN A DOG—IT'S UNFAIR TO THE DOG.

DUMB DOG!

AUTHOR'S NOTE: An acquaintance upon hearing a dog owner tell how his dog greeted him most eagerly after merely ten minutes absence, remarked "Dogs certainly are dumb." The remark induced us to write this poem Dumb Dog.

He feign would drop to slumber deep and sound
But you, your smallest move, he needs must watch.
Down in the cool and quiet cellar, bed is kept for him—
Yet by your side in hot and stifling room, he gasps content.

DUMB DOG, DUMB DOG, DUMB DOG!

Your talk is boresome, vile your manners too;
Yet eager mouth and eyes he ever shows to you.
You sit alone and sad—your friends no longer care;
But not alone—your dog is there, unknowing change.

DUMB DOG, DUMB DOG, DUMB DOG!

You may be right; you may be wrong;
A secret sin may gnaw your soul;
The world your guilt or crime may ask.
Your dog brisk wags the same gay tail.

DUMB DOG, DUMB DOG, DUMB DOG!

The loyalty you held abiding in your friends
Has fled; your wealth gone too, betrays their tinsel worth.
Your mind in stealth entices fear of self-brought death—
But no! you feel a soft moist nose against your hand.

DUMB DOG, DUMB DOG, DUMB DOG!

My Dog is Dead

There lies his ball; I wait to see him pounce
And shake it in mock fight which pleases
him.
I thot I heard his quick light step again
In playful trot on stairway up and down.

The leash hangs on the wall; I'll shake it
loud,
Then joyfully he'll bound into the room
Impatient for his romp. He does not come—
No wistful face peers thru half-open door.

The rugs lie smooth; the curtains are not
torn.
I haven't missed a shoe or rag today.
The house is dreadful still, until I wish
I heard four feet come pitpat down the hall.

The soft moist nose that pushed against my
hand
The paw that touched me to demand its
wish,
The pleading lively eye, the plaintive bark—
What sweet annoyances they now would
seem!

The door is open and the gate ajar;
No need to close them—he will not run out.
That new ball throw away; I bought it for
His next birthday—but he will never
know.

The Old Dog

The old dog sleeps before the fire
Content to doze the hours away.
His step now drags uncertainly
Where once he frisked 'mid bark and play

Long lies he in the warming sun—
The hunter home from faroff hills,
To run his last and losing race
As eyes grow dim and legs give way.

Keen life still clings within his frame
Yet 'tis but trace of other days
As mem'ry's musings run the chase
In years when legs were swift and strong.

He's deep asleep while muffled bark,
The twitching nose and treading feet
Waft him in dreams across the fields
On trails of game and new-found scent.

Tonight you softly pat his head
As blinking eyes are quick to close.
You miss his wonted nudge and bark
When morning finds him still asleep.

You call—he does not open eye
Or wag that ever cheerful tail;
You think him merely sleeping sound—
And soon to leap up joyfully.

Alas, the stiff and stretched out legs,
The breathless loin, the glassy eye
Which oft so soft and moist did plead,
Tell now that death has found its mark!

The brave, stout heart beats now no more
To warm the body whose sole thot
Knew only your command as law—
A servant for your ev'ry wish.

A noble soul has fled the earth,
Which never knew deceit nor guile;
Of man was part, a better part,
Without his treach'rous smile and face.

High up at heaven's gate he waits
Without complaint tho long the hours—
An ear pricked up, half-opened eye
To catch quick sight when master comes.

At last a loved familiar face
The watchful dog discerns with joy.
"What sound is that?" the master asks
In strange surprise. No need to wait—

The answer comes in leap and bark—
Old dog, old master once again
Unite to never part as both
In gladsome pace wend way to God.

Be Not So Cruel

Have you forgotten that attack by night
When my sharp bark and sudden forward
plunge,
The robber's gun quick whirled aside, and
forth
Did drive the evil ones who sought your
death?

THEN BE NOT SO CRUEL WITH YOUR BLOWS!

Is not the time but scarce a scant full moon
When unaware to all who loved her dear
Swift wheels bore down upon your only
child—
But my firm mouth safe snatched her from
the street?

THEN BE NOT SO CRUEL WITH YOUR BLOWS!

Not always fortune's smile has been your
lot.
My mind recalls your grief and lonesome
want.
Who then save me your dog awaited you
With honest love, full faith and heart
content?

THEN BE NOT SO CRUEL WITH YOUR BLOWS!

I am your dog and you my greatest god.
The world is yours, had I the world to give.
I only ask a slight return for all
My love that's yours tho death demand its
proof.

THEN BE NOT SO CRUEL WITH YOUR BLOWS!

FROM A COLOURED PRINT IN CYNOGRAPHIA BRITANNICA (SYDENHAM EDWARDS) PUBLISHED IN 1803.

Dogs, Too, Get Spring Fever

In all lands the return of warming sunshine brings the pleasing spring fever. Dogs too are its willing victims. They find increasing delight in their daily vagabonding. The plain, soft earth after a winter of concealment under the snow, presents myriads of new smells; and as anyone initiated into the inner cult of dog lore can tell you, the hors d'oeuvres of a canine menu are the multitude of smells awaiting detection by the dog's nose in every spot and space.

The paws of the dog itch to be soothed by digging in the once-again soft ground of springtime. A nabor's lawn has just been dedicated with the planting of flower seeds and shrubbery after a winter of ecstatic reading of the alluring seed catalogs by the hopeful nabor.

Beware—you will incur your good nabor's enmity! Act before it is too late! Be certain that your dog harkens to your voice, else you will need to retrieve him in the front yard next door happily scratching up the earth and grass with all fours and looking at you with a devil-may-care, "haven't we got fun?" expression.

It's his forgivable way of expressing spring fever. But—call him quickly and hide yourself away before your neighbor's wife spots you out of the front window. Walk nonchalantly as if you never owned a dog in your life.

And have your wife send to your neighbor's wife that evening as a peace offering, some delicacy she has just cooked, for dogs will be dogs, especially in springtime.

The Dog's Bill of Rights

I. I want nutritious food once daily—not too much; and don't believe the old idea that bones are good for me.

II. I want clean water in a clean dish twice daily.

III. I want a dry, ventilated but draftless place for sleeping.

IV. I want a collar that doesn't choke me or isn't so loose it catches on my head.

V. I want a quiet place in the basement on the Fourth of July.

VI. I want every boy reprimanded but softly, who throws stones at me or twists my ears.

VII. I want folks to judge me as a dog and from a dog's viewpoints.

VIII. I want everybody to keep in mind that I do with my mouth, most things they do with their hands; so, they needn't be afraid of a dog's teeth.

IX. I want to be treated sympathetically, just as I treat small children and all those in distress, who belong to my master's clan.

X. I want my mind and body trained so that I can be of the fullest service.

XI. I want to be considered one of the family, for I will give my life to protect it.

XII. I want my master to be my god on earth and to act the part.

SIGNED: for all dogs:

FIDO.

Doggrams

One of the reasons we could wish that dogs could talk is that they might tell us their opinion of humans.

A puppy becomes housebroken in manners in twenty days but some folks don't in twenty years.

If some people we know owned appropriate breeds of dogs, they'd be leading polecats on leashes.

If every dog owner were as good human as his dog is good dog, the devil would go bankrupt.

If dogs could talk, it would be bad manners in polite dog society to call a dog a man.

The neurotic, undependable dog is a four-legged shadow of his owner.

Who kicks a dog thereby kicks his own soul into hell.

I don't trust a man who kicks or beats a dog.

Judge a man's character best by the way he treats his dog.

CH. "BRENDON BERYL".

This is one of Mrs. Adlam's noted bitches, and its longer legs and general difference in build will be recognized in comparison with "Num Skull".

The Seven Advantages of Owning a Pedigreed Dog

Briefly summarized, these are the seven advantages of owning a purebred dog. Ownership becomes a matter of pride, of property value and income, plus pleasure in ownership.

It is true that a dog is a dog the world around and that the dogs themselves know nothing about pedigrees. However, there is a difference, because most of our dog problems, including that of rabies, the dog pound and nabors' complaints arise out of acts of mixed-bred or just plain dogs.

1. The pedigreed (purebred) dog, first of all, costs anywhere from $25 to $75 as a three-months puppy.

The very fact that the owner has a substantial investment in his purchase, causes him to take some care of his property and give it attention.

2. The owner of a pedigreed dog has a dog because he wants it; and not because some nabor wishing to get rid of a litter of mongrel puppies, prevails upon him to take one of the "cute little things," which will develop into something not so cute.

3. The pedigreed dog has distinct individuality, in that his ancestry or pedigree is a known matter and can be recorded in a national registration or stud book.

4. The pedigreed dog is a known product, in that the disposition, habits and background of the dog are definitely known. These are in the main just like those of all members of his breed. There is no such uniformity nor assurance in the mongrel or mixed-bred dogs.

5. The pedigreed dog is a trademarked, brand-stamped article. The purchaser knows what he is getting, not only in disposition and manners as stated, but also in bloodlines. He can breed to another dog of the same breed and sell the puppies in advance, because he knows the puppies will be like their parents—purebred, of the same breed. They in turn can carry on with offspring exactly of the same type.

6. A pedigreed dog, more particularly a bitch, can be bred and thus an additional income derived from the sale of the puppies.

7. It does not cost any more to care for and train a pedigreed dog than a mixed-bred dog. The upkeep is the same for either one.

Postscript—Fortunately the dogs themselves know nothing about pedigrees and the lowliest mongrel considers himself as good and a doggone site better than the loftiest show champion.

Seventeen Training Don'ts

Sometimes what should be done can be said best by telling what should not be done. The reasons for the don'ts should be evident to every person in process of training his dog. Each one is based upon the basic psychology of the dog's mind.

1. DON'T punish your dog while you are angry or lack control of yourself.

2. DON'T punish your dog with the lead or any instrument of training or anything he should associate with duty or pleasure.

3. DON'T sneak up on your dog, grab him from the rear, surprise him or reach for him quickly.

4. DON'T chase your dog to catch him; he must come to you or follow after you.

5. DON'T coax your dog to you and then turn upon him with punishment. You will regret the deception.

6. DON'T trick, fool or taunt your dog. It is cruel and inconsistent to tease your dog to come to you when he can not.

7. DON'T punish a dog by stepping on his paws needlessly. They are exceedingly sensitive. Don't twist his ears playfully or otherwise. Don't strike him on the backbone, in the face or on the ears.

8. DON'T nag your dog; don't be giving orders to him constantly; don't pester him with your shoutings.

9. DON'T praise a dog for doing a certain act, then at a later time,

scold him for doing the same act. Consistency on your part is a chief virtue in dog training.

10. DON'T train your dog within an hour after he has eaten.

11. DON'T ever lose patience with a puppy younger than six months and seldom with a dog older.

12. DON'T throw or kick a puppy nor lift him by the head or leg or skin of the neck.

13. DON'T work your dog without some short rest or play periods during training lesson. A five-minute rest for every twenty minutes of training is desirable. Feats requiring strength and endurance are for a dog older than six months.

14. DON'T permit everyone and anyone to give commands to your dog. While you are training him, he must be a one-man dog, depending on you to feed him and care for him.

15. DON'T consider tricks the chief purpose in training. Usefulness is the object sought in all instruction of the dog. Acts that spring naturally from the dog's instincts are to be fostered.

16. DON'T expect your dog to be a wonderful dog after a few weeks of training; four months to a year may be necessary in order to make the master proud of him, but the work is worth the effort. Training never ends.

17. DON'T jump to the conclusion that your dog is dumb. He may differ with you, believing the trainer should know more than the dog.

"I WANT ALL THE BOOKS YOU HAVE ON DOG TRAINING!"

30 DON'TS FOR EVERY DOG OWNER

I am going to tell you some of the things a dog owner should NOT do. Most of my "Don'ts" may seem arbitrary, but they are sound advice.

DON'T surprise a sleeping dog nor approach any dog without giving him notice.
DON'T make a sissy of your dog by coddling him.
DON'T allow the dog to become chilled after bathing.
DON'T give worm medicine to a sick dog.
DON'T exercise the dog within thirty minutes after he has eaten.
DON'T allow strangers to chastise the dog.
DON'T fear a dog merely because he is frothing at the mouth.
DON'T allow the dog to lie constantly near the radiator in winter.
DON'T fondle or pet strange dogs.
DON'T give quantities of water to a dog that is vomiting.
DON'T allow dogs to sit in any and all chairs in the home.
DON'T take dogs needlessly into strange kennels as there is danger of disease.
DON'T allow the dog to roam by himself; he should always be within sight of his master.
DON'T beat a dog; a light stroke with a few loosely rolled sheets of newspaper plus shaming with the voice generally are sufficient.
DON'T believe that eating of meat by the dog will make it "go mad."
DON'T give castor oil for all forms of constipation.
DON'T neglect paying (and promptly too) for damages your dog may have done.
DON'T pour kerosene on a dog's skin for killing fleas.
DON'T neglect calling a veterinarian promptly for your sick dog, since both dog and doctor want to live.
DON'T encourage needless dog fights.
DON'T attempt to take a bone away from a dog without first calling his attention to yourself; never interfere with a strange dog while it is eating.
DON'T feed any very small or sharp-pointed bones.
DON'T let your dog sleep in a draft or in a damp place.
DON'T let everybody pet your dog if he is to be a watchdog.
DON'T shout commands to your dog in an excited tone of voice.

DON'T kill your dog by overfeeding him.

DON'T run the risk of losing your dog by not having your name and address on his collar plate.

DON'T try to avoid paying a dog license fee.

DON'T let your dog cross the street without being by your side, even if well trained, or on lead.

DON'T believe everything poorly informed people tell you about dogs.—

A Dozen Dog Care Do's

1. Trim toenails every three months with heavy scissors or regular nail trimmer.
2. Have a set day each month for examining your dog externally inch by inch, including "smelling the ears"
3. Brush or wipe the teeth and gums with a soft cloth weekly and weakly, either dry or slightly soaked in salt-and-soda water solution.
4. Watch the frequency, color and consistency of bowel movements as symptom of ailing condition.
5. Feed your dog each day at the same scheduled hour and spot, and in the same food pan.
6. Brush your dog with a not-too-soft brush vigorously every day, no matter how lazy you yourself feel.
7. Take your dog and yourself out for three romps a day, one of which should be extra long.
8. Keep your dog, no matter how well trained, on a lead and close to you, (on your left) when on busy streets and in crowds.
9. Sun and air the dog's bedding once a week.
10. Cure a skin disease at first notice and before it has a chance to intensify.
11. Prolong your dog's life by keeping him away from the dinner table at mealtime and from eating frequently.
12. Have patience with your dog just as he 'puts up' with you. Be sympathetic with his limitations.

PRESIDENT AND VICTORIA
Two early importations shown by the late E. Sheffield Porter

SIR WM. VERNER S TARQUIN
Shown at New York in 1880

OLD DUTCH
Fred Hinks' great sire, a pillar of the Stud Book

BRUTUS
Painted by Edwin Cooper and published in the "Sporting Magazine"

CHAMPION MAGGIE MAY
One of Mr. Frank Doles' old winners and producers

VENOM
Published in 1831 in the "Sporting Magazine"

IF DOGS WERE MASTERS

The Dog Gives Training Advice to His Master

Now, look here, human; I realize you've got to know more than the dog before you can teach him, but please mix common sense and good judgment with your knowledge.

I can't talk with words. You can teach me to lie down with the command UP. The big job you have in this training work with me as your pupil is to get your ideas across to me. Don't worry about my end of it, if I can figure out in my dog mind what you want me to do.

And incidentally, nine times of ten a dog disobeys, he isn't actually doing that—he just doesn't get what you had in mind. Believe me, we dogs have only one big act on our program—to win your approval in everything we do. I know it's misplaced devotion at times but we'll skip that.

Just remember, master, that we are dogs—and glad of it too. We aren't humans and don't want to be. To us this is a dog's world, mostly of smells and sounds. We don't want to be called humans—that's unfair to us.

But when you map out a training course look at it from the dog's viewpoint. Does the act appeal to our love of play, our desire to please, our interest in getting something to eat, our curiosity in seeing what's happening on the other side of the fence? Put a canine angle on your training efforts—and we'll respond. We want to be all dog, and not half human.

Do you recall the famous court case in which Sam Smith was tried for shooting a dog that leaped over his fence, dug up his garden, and bit one of the Smith children badly? Well, the jury convicted Smith but we dogs took a vote and decided that the dog's owner should have been found guilty instead.

When one of us is taken to the pound in the dog catcher's truck and there murdered legally if no one reclaims us, our blood is on the soul of the owner who thot so little of us that he did not keep us under his control.

And why shouldn't we in turn set forth the essential qualities of a successful trainer? We want our trainers to possess an abundance of FOUR things:

1. Patience with its twin selfcontrol.
2. Seriousness of purpose, for the trainer is moulding our characters; and this seriousness demands that he concentrate on his training work similarly as he requires us.
3. Consistency of methods and aims, so that we will not be confused or deceived.
4. Sincere love for us dogs.

I might bark in passing that we laugh in our paw when you humans, our assumed gods, lose your temper over us, shout commands excitedly, are inconsistent in not sticking to the same command for the same obedience or let us get away with pretended deafness when you speak to us.

At any rate, just look at things thru our eyes and minds; make yourself one of us for the time being when you are training us—you don't really train us—we can do all this sort of stuff naturally; you're just kind of dumb in getting it out of us.

Signed — — for all dogs
FIDO

An Apology for the Dog Catcher

On our way to the office the other day, a black delivery truck, of the panel type, ground its wheels and came to a sudden halt in the middle of the busy street. "That's strange," we thot to ourselves.

Three young men (all policemen) leaped out of the same seat—and as one of them threw something ahead of him, we heard the shriek of a dog.

Then we knew—the dog catchers, at work on Chicago's southside. The truck bore the lettering—Chicago Municipal Animal Shelter—Truck No. 1.

The agonized high-pitched screams of the dog increased. He was running toward us—a mongrel dog of the large foxterrier type, white with black markings. A second man rushed in front of him, threw a rounded shining copper wire toward the dog, but missed. It was of loop type, which tightened at one end into a smaller, choke collar thrown over an object and the one end pulled back.

Racing at top speed, the dog outdistanced them down the street—and inwardly we were glad. All our theory and propaganda went askew. We almost shouted out "Ha, Ha, he got away."

But our gladness vanished quickly as the truck pulled away, for at the open lattice work of the rear, we saw at least six dogs peering thru, with wide, frightened, wondering eyes.

Likely to all these six dogs—and additional ones ensnared later, the lettering on the truck was in error—not Municipal Animal SHELTER but Municipal Animal MURDERING.

We cannot join those who everlastingly are damning the dog catcher. He may be a kindhearted person who loves dogs; but his unpleasant work is made necessary by dog owners rather than the dogs themselves.

A license to own a dog does not give the owner of the license the privilege of having his dog roam the countryside or the public streets. The law against wandering dogs applies equally to licensed and unlicensed dogs.

A dog can lead a happy life in the city if properly cared for, without becoming a pillager of garbage cans, a destroyer of nabors' grounds, and a menace to traffic by crossing the road as cars approach.

We do not plead for more dogs, but for better dog owners and better care for the dogs we already have.

Dog owners rather than the dogs should be licensed and a searching examination be given to applicants for dog licenses to ascertain whether or not they are the right kind of people to own dogs.

There shouldn't be any stray dogs. There shouldn't be any dogs roaming away from their owners or custodians. Stray dogs cause 95% of our dog problems, and certainly 99% of our rabies problems.

But it's the nature of the species to move about, to visit here and there, to roam for the pleasure of it. The stray dog itself is not to be condemned because it is a stray. It is not doing anything which even remotely to its mind, it can consider criminal or unnatural.

The wrong animals were in the dog catcher's truck. Behind the iron grating should have been the owners of these six dogs—careless, indifferent, unappreciative persons who never should own dogs because they are unworthy of them and the responsibility dog ownership entails.

Every stray dog put to death in the dog pound (and only one of every eight is reclaimed) is murdered; for he comes to his death not thru any wrongdoing of his. He did not violate any canine criminal code.

He is killed because the one he trusted, the one to whom he gave the world's greatest example of loyalty and devotion, his master, didn't care. The dog's blood should rest tormentedly upon the conscience of the owner—but unfortunately in most cases it doesn't.

Don't look down on the dog catcher. He is a citizen doing his duty as a law enforcer.

Hurl your condemnation at the persons who make his job necessary—the millions of dog owners who do not control, care for or train their dogs, the people who indirectly are murderers of their dogs.

I have difficulty in liking otherwise good people who do not like dogs.

CH. "NUM SKULL".

It is difficult in a few words to describe the correct Bull Terrier and just as difficult to point the faults of an excellent specimen. Even champions vary to some extent, as will be seen if we compare Mr. H. L. Summer's "Num Skull" with the picture above.

Cats versus Dogs

We like cats. They furnish running exercise for dogs and always win the race. They are a living, moving thing of beauty, softness and grace. They and the birds are among the few animals that wash themselves.

Like the dog, they are a heritage from the wilderness. But whereas Fido the dog has made an almost complete adjustment between savagery and civilization, Pussy the cat clings to most of her ancestors' ways.

She is still a member of her ancient race of tigers, lions and panthers. She is a tiger of small size who deigns to favor you with her presence in your house, sleeping haughtily at your very fireplace. She permits you to occupy the house with her. Her lair demands her loyalty for she prefers it even tho the family moves away.

She moves with all the proudness of her proud race. One would think that such diminutive descendant of the lion and the tiger would be marked with humility. Her very whiskers, pure relic of the jungle and its shadows, exude haughtiness. She washes herself publicly that all may see the rite of the elite.

She likes the darkness; her paths are those of the night; the stars evoke the melody of her soul (on these nocturnal romantic occasions, more commonly "his" soul).

She travels alone. Who has seen a pack of cats? Secrecy confided to no one, is her abiding trait.

Behind those greenish-yellow gleaming eyes, guarded by pupils now round, now but an upright slit, reside mystery, adventure, and dark plannings.

She possesses a most uncertain disposition. Her set countenance staring at your face shamelessly, may mean friendliness or a scratch. That gracefully agile tail may be but a salute to those about to die. She is a daughter of many moods, royal in her fits of temper.

Where the cat is a pet, the dog is a companion. Where the cat is a lady, the dog is a roustabout. Where the cat is disdainful, the dog is a good fellow. Where the cat is unconcerned with its mistress, the dog imitates the moods of his master.

We use "she" when speaking of cats but refer to the dog as "he" and could there be more conclusive proof of what we are trying to argue than this natural choice of pronoun in the third person?

MODESTY

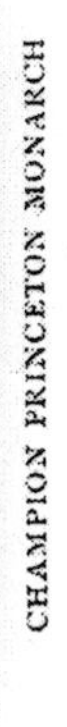

CHAMPION PRINCETON MONARCH

CHAMPION CARNEY

WENTWORTH BRANT

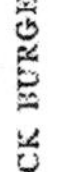

DICK BURGE

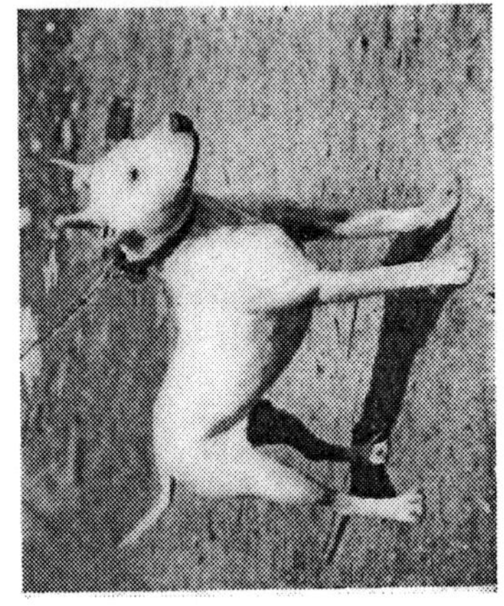

EDGEWOOD PENN

RANCOCAS GINGER

Property of Mr. H. Tatnall Brown

EDGEWOOD J. P. H.

Property of Mr. W. Freeland Kendrick

CH. FAULTLESS OF THE POINT

Property of Mr. Clair Foster

CH. BLOOMSBURY BURGE

A specimen uncropped English dog

CH. EDGEWOOD CRYSTAL

Formerly the property of Mr. F. F. Dole

CH. AJAX OF THE POINT

Property of Mr. Clair Foster

Have a Heart, Mr. Dog Owner

The following written by the author applies to the puppy just purchased, perhaps from a distant kennel, and now arrived in the home of its new owner. Most puppies are purchased "at a distance," and at the tender age of about four months.

NOTHING is more pathetic and at the same time more courageous than a few-months-old puppy literally pulled away from its mother, from its brothers and sisters; then pushed into a crate, shaken up on a jolting journey, finally to be ushered into the presence of strangers in its new home, whose selection certainly has been without its choice or knowledge.

THE SLATS are torn off the crate—a commotion enuf to terrify even an old dog. The little breathing bunch of softness is cold, hungry, trembling after the roughness of travel, and with it all, a sickness it never knew before—that of loneliness.

FAR FROM HOME and playmates, and the world it has known, it peers out of the crate with frightened yet trusting eyes.

IT LOOKS ABOUT only to be disappointed for it had fancied dimly in its baby mind, that in some way, at the end of the journey, mother and the rest of the family would be there to welcome it with a pretended sniff of curiosity and then would resume the customary play.

THE PAT OF a hand, a saucer of milk, a few softly spoken words, and almost a miracle transpires.

THE TAIL WAGS. The eyes become less drawn; they look up at you with a sort of soulful pleading. The legs wobble a bit, then walk.

THE CRATE, THE trembling and the unfriendly world are forgotten. The pup begins to explore the new home, every crack and corner—and ten days later, owns the house and everything in it, including yourself.

CH. WOODCOTE WONDER.

In Praise of the Female

NOTWITHSTANDING that prejudice often prefers her brother, the female dog has all the virtues of her species and fewer of the vices. Indeed it may be said that she excels the male in most of the good qualities which have endeared the dog to us as man's best friend.

IN A DOG we demand companionship, watchful guarding and usefulness as the occasion requires. These the female gives in greater measure and more gracefully than does the male.

HER COMPANIONSHIP is mellowed with a devotion more steadfast and gentle, ever given with the subtle charm of her sex.

SHE IS A keener watcher, feels a more constant sense of duty, and with motherly suspicion, discriminates more carefully between friend of the family and the stranger.

THE HOUSEWIFE has less trouble with conduct, fewer pieces of bric-a-brac to mend, and less sweeping to do.

HER GOOD manners are evident in the finesse with which she eats, in contrast to the male's greedy gulping.

IF HOUSEBREAKING can be regarded as a nasty task, choose the female—she is cleaner in the home, does her duties less frequently, and outdoors surely does them more modestly and over smaller area.

THE FEMALE is a homebody, jealous of the family possessions, whereas her brother may incline to be the tramp. The guilt of digging up a neighbor's flowers usually must be placed upon the roaming male.

THE FEMALE is less presumptuous unless it be with children; in them she assumes a motherly interest. She senses danger more quickly. The extra attention she pays to the baby of the household reveals an instinctive solicitude for the weak and helpless.

TRAINERS PREFER the female for she learns more quickly and keeps her mind on the task at hand. Her conscience is more sensitive to disobedience. On game in the field, she is fully as keen and successful.

WHEREAS THE male is in season all the year, the female comes into heat only twice a year and then for a scarce twenty days; she asks only that she be kept at home or, if outdoors, on a lead, during these brief periods.

IN NOTHING ELSE is the prejudice against the female dog (let us not hesitate to call her openly by the ancient and honorable name of bitch) so evident and unfair as with regard to her heat. When she has matured and in turn is ready to repeat the divine mystery of birth, she is shunned, almost cursed as tho her sex were a plague, as tho she should be punished for her sex and for the creative duties Nature has decreed for all of her sex in all species of animal life.

IN PUREBRED breeding, the female is just as important (and not a few authorities of heredity declare her more dominant) as the stud male; her pedigree is to be studied just as carefully.

FURTHER SHE has the advantage of motherhood; it is she who carries the allotment of coming life. She can be mated and thereby add her bit to the family's income thru presenting her owner with duplicates of herself to carry on in other homes.

LOGICALLY INDEED the female is to be preferred to the male, and the prospective purchaser of a puppy well can place the advantage with her in making his choice.

Why Own a Dog

THAT you may not forget how to play as exemplified by the dog, who carries his puppy heart on thru into the graying muzzle—

THAT you may have for your home and possessions an alert burglar alarm and a policeman who never sleeps—

THAT you may be reminded daily and with resultant humility that you and the animal kingdom are of one and the same group in the scheme of creation—

THAT you may live above petty selfishness thru obligating yourself for the welfare of one who depends implicitly upon you and never complains if you are derelict—

THAT you may forget the worries of the day and the strain of its routine as arriving home, you are greeted with unfeigned delight by one whose heart is filled only with thot of you and whose existence, he believes, cannot go on apart from yours—

THAT you may find surcease from being bored thru observing the dog's freshness in doing the customary little things, his curiosity over the flutter of a leaf to the ground, and his discovery of new delights along old paths—

THAT your children, growing up with a dog, may see a daily living sermon on kindness, obligation to others and the necessity for obedience, and that later they can translate these qualities into good citizenship.

THAT you may learn from your servant the dog to live with faith in fellowmen, with a readiness to forgive, and above all, with an unselfishness which may not be logical but is divinely refreshing—

THAT by your dog's contagious example, you may live each day to its fullness, be always ready for new adventure, and find zest in common and uncommon things alike—

THAT all these things may come to pass.

GET A DOG—

OWN A DOG—

AND BE OWNED BY A DOG.

THEY SHOULDN'T OWN DOGS

Are there too many dogs? Perhaps yes, perhaps no. But here we discuss the question—are there too many undesirable dog owners?

Many years ago (1928) National Dog Week began with the slogan—'a dog in every home.' Little time was required to realize that this slogan was not a good one. Today the canine population averages about one dog in every two of five families. All of us connected with the Week soon discovered that our enthusiasm was not founded upon reality.

A hasty check-up of dogs on the street, of stray and unwanted dogs, shows clearly that most dog problems such as control, rabies, stock damages, biters, alley roamers, street fights, and the like are blameable against the roaming dog; and that in most cases, he is owned by someone who just doesn't care, who considers dog ownership 'just one of those things.'

Even some owners who have paid the annual license fee harbor the idea that having paid the fee, therefore their dogs have extra privileges, including that of running the streets. Frankly, about the only thing a dog license fee gives the owner is the right not to be arrested for not taking out a license for owning the dog.

Here I enumerate some of the kinds of dog owners who are not too desirable, and some of whom for the sake of their dogs, should not own dogs.

THE FAMILY who gets a dog because it is fashionable to have a dog.

THE OWNER who denounces inoculation against rabies, yet permits his dog to run at large.

THE LAZY DOG owner—he who doesn't give the dog a brushing, grooming or bath—and if the weather is a bit rainy, cloudy, chilly, does not take the dog out for a run.

THE INCONSIDERATE dog owner—he who permits his dog to leap up on other persons, paw their clothes, nip hosiery.

THE DOG OWNER who permits his dog to bark incessantly when he is away from the house; or bark at all hours of the day and night.

THE PRETENDER—he who makes a show of kindness before visitors but neglects to give the dog exercise, or sober care.

THE UNNEIGHBORLY dog owner—he permits his dog to roam streets, alleys, gardens and lawns, doing damage.

THE UNKIND DOG owner—he who fails to take his sick dog to the veterinarian, or who waits too long before doing so.

Breeder's Code

1. I will study the bitch as well as the sire.
2. I will study grandparents rather than parents.
3. I will not pay attention to breeding superstitions.
4. I will interpret a pedigree by breeding facts and dominance rather than by names and titles.
5. I will keep full breeding records and draw conclusions accordingly.
6. I will put away culls, weaklings and the deformed shortly after birth.
7. I will not breed, sell or give away a shy or excessively nervous dog.
8. I will judge a stud by his offspring even to the third generation.
9. I will honor most the bred-by-exhibitor dog.
10. I will give preference to breeding specimens of good temperament and strong nerves.
11. I will have patience to try again and again, and will not be discouraged by litters which are disappointments.
12. I will be led on constantly by the seductive dream of one day producing the perfect dog of my breed, and if another breeder forges ahead of me, I shall envy but also praise him.

The Dogist's Code

(Note—Henry L. Mencken in his Dictionary of American Language Vol. II., credits the author Will Judy with the origin of the word dogist.)

I. Color all your work with a deep love for all dogs.

II. Be sympathetic counselor to the novice for you yourself once knew as little as he.

III. Beware of him who is quick to find fault for likely you will be his target in time.

IV. Say nothing rather than out of malice, speak ill of another kennel or breed.

V. Seek business on your own merit rather than by taking it away from a competitor.

VI. Envy the competitor who forges ahead of you, but praise him also.

VII. Win with a smile of course, but to lose with a smile lessens the defeat and requires greater sportsmanship.

VIII. When you lose, resolve to come back to win at a later time.

IX. Show in yourself the same sportsmanship you demand of others.

X. Be the god-on-earth and all-wise master your dogs think you are.

The Spirit of Sportsmanship

(A word of counsel to exhibitors at dog shows)

Dog shows are fascinating, thrilling, interesting. They afford opportunity for social contacts, for friendly gatherings, for sportsmen to gather from all sections of America. To win a blue or even the second red in strong competition gives deep pleasure.

The dogs themselves receive the best of care; in truth, most of them enjoy going away from the kennels to be posed in the show ring.

A dog may win against another mostly because he presents his good points to better advantage before the judge; he is "on his toes," properly posed for his particular breed. At tomorrow's show he may lose to the same dog.

If you have what you consider a typy specimen, enter him at one or more dog shows to get an official opinion thru the AKC licensed judge.

If you win, smile; if you lose, smile; and in either case, let your smile be sincere. One of the chief marks of a true sportsman is his conduct in time of defeat.

The placing of your dog at one show is only one man's opinion of your dog—the judge's, and on that particular day, it is official for that show. But the next show, another judge, liking your type of dog, and under different competition, may place your dog first. Few good dogs go thru to the title without losing perhaps two of every five times.

One dog show does not make or break a dog. Some great winners were defeated at their first show.

Of course, you have the best dog in the world, until you meet another dog owner, and he will tell you that he has the best dog in the world. Both of you will be mostly right.

Necessity for Good Dog Books

Dog books are like tools—they are necessary; they furnish valuable information; they give the benefit of the judgment and experience of experts of this and other days. Without them, we would be as a needlewoman working in the dark.

Just as it is a duty to the fancy that the dog fancier subscribe to one or more good dog magazines, so also it is his personal obligation that he purchase books about his breed. Unless enough books can be sold to render a profit to the author and the publisher, few dog books will be available in the future

The publication of a worthy book on a breed enhances the popularity of the particular breed, adds recruits to its fancy, and makes possible the much-desired uniformity in type and breeding by setting forth tried and correct rules and procedure, along with a record of what has been accomplished in the past and what it is hoped to accomplish in the future.

The dog fancier's library should be filled with books on his own breed and with a wide selection of general books on the dog. The successful fancier in breeding, in the show ring, and elsewhere is always the well-read fancier.

Ch. Charlwood Victor-Wild.

The Most Unusual Dog Cemetery in the World

On a journey of ours thru Scotland in June 1949, we of course stopt at Edinburgh and visited the Edinburgh Castle set high on the hill as perfect as in any storybook picture.

At the War Memorial here, we noted that the sculptor has included the war dog (German shepherd) as one of those who did his part in the First World War. This Memorial should rank among the world's greatest attainments of art.

We were looking down from the ramp into the valley far below, when our eye chanced to see on a turret below us, the sign CEMETERY FOR SOLDIERS' DOGS.

Here was a plat hardly more than 20 ft. long. We were greatly touched with this scene, especially by the graves. Each grave was marked with a small tombstone. One bore the inscription "Don—1866." Another stone read: "Flora, Canteen Pet, 1885." "Chips" had a small stone dated 1897. There were Flory, Yum Yum, Charley, Billie Tinker, Little Tim, Pat Marut, all buried here. The latest comer was "Scamp, faithful chum of Jack Wilson Patterson, June 1947."

We counted 23 graves in this most unusual dog cemetery in the world—a cemetery on top of a tower in a high castle. It is a tribute to the soldiers who owned these dogs and to the dogs themselves—

WE DO NOT OWN OUR DOGS; THEY OWN US

No investment pays such large and constant dividends as the purchase of a dog. In service and companionship, the dog is a constantly paying investment over a period of years.

On the average, a dog for 7 to 10 years pays daily dividends in loyalty, watchfulness and service.

There is still another important consideration to this investment—there is no depreciation. In fact, the investment increases in intrinsic value until the day of death. His heart remains ever young, however, gray his muzzle, slow his step.

The dog is the only instance where money can buy true love.

You may own a dog but he really owns you; he places his investment of devotion in you, as his master.

It is sometimes uncertain whether you or your dog is the master for he often has his way against your will and yet not so. Often one is heard to say, "I own this dog" when it would really be more proper to say, "This dog owns me."

DOG SHOW IMPRESSIONS

Barking—catalog seller shouting—sawdust—people conversing in groups—gaily-gowned women—more humans chattering—ribbons everywhere—barking—table of trophies—dogs pulling on leads—superintendent explaining to a deaf woman why her entry was omitted—serious looking judges—barking—dog crates—beautiful women—pekes barking at danes—antiseptic sprayed on sawdust—barking—yelping—barking—dogs sleeping on cushions—friends greeting one another—fat men leading chihuahuas—wives leading husbands—beginners explaining show secrets to oldtimers—barking—argument at door about a pass—chief steward running six ways at one time—glamorous exhibitor smiling at judge—more chattering by humans—barking—dog magazine solicitor extolling his publication at so much per year—winner of yellow ribbon parading joyfully back and forth—losers' alibis—checking out the crates—exhibitor demonstrating why his dog should have won—barking—lights out—final bark—final final bark.—

GREATER DELITES ENJOYED BY TRAINED DOG AND HIS OWNER

Rather than to have more dogs, the slogan should be—"better dogs and better care for them." Better dogs includes a greater development of mental abilities; and better care includes physical welfare of course, but also proper training so that the dog of his own accord can meet the various situations which confront him.

Behind the expressive and pleading brown eyes and within the skull of the dog lies a brain which has untold possibilities; these need to be developed so that the companionship and the understanding between man and his dog may be deeper and indeed be spiritual. Dogs must give an account of themselves and their opportunities, but it is unjust to demand thi if their masters do not train their minds.

A world of pleasure and usefulness can be gotten from the trained dog. His obedience to the spoken word, his quick compliance, give delight to all who behold him. His training raises him to a higher level so that he seems not a beast of the field but a companion worthy to walk by the side of man, the only god he knows.—

"Ten Commandments" for the Dog Owner

The dog's god on earth is his owner. I use this phrase "god on earth" because it stresses the important point that the dog is a prisoner—a willing one, of course —to the human race. He is a devoted slave and follower, without the ability to argue terms or demand better treatment.

The fact that the dog is not a free agent emphasizes the responsibility of every owner to his dog. The very health, comfort, and life of the dog are dependent upon his owner. As the tempo of our modern life is intensified, this four-footed transplantation from the wilds becomes even more dependent upon his overlord —his "god on earth."

The following ten suggestions, cautions and advice appear to me to be worthy of recognition as the "Ten Commandments" for the conscientious dog owner.

I. Give your dog a monthly physical examination: check his skin for possible irritation; "smell" the inside of his ears for possible canker infection. Every six months have his toe nails cut and teeth cleaned.

II. On snowy, rainy, slushy days, have a large, rough, absorbent towel just inside the door, within reach. Use it vigorously to clean, wipe, and dry the dog down to the skin—especially between the toes—when he comes back from his romp outdoors.

III. When you have guests in the house, make certain the dog does not paw the ladies' stockings; does not leap on the guests; does not make a nuisance of himself in any way.

IV. At least every two days, brush the dog's coat thoroughly—brush tenderly around ears and head. Make certain the bristles of the brush reach down to the skin in order to remove dandruff and other impurities.

V. Train your dog so that he knows his place in the house. It is never in the dining room while you are eating; never sleeping against the radiator, nor at top or bottom of stairways, nor in hallways. Have a definite place designated for him where to eat and sleep.

VI. Regard your dog as a dog and not as half-human; no "baby talk," no coddling.

VII. Do not wait until it is too late to take your dog to the veterinarian. Both the dog and the doctor want to live.

VIII. Have regard for your nabors and their rights and wishes by keeping your dog under control so that he does not damage their lawns or cause them annoyance.

IX. Do not permit your dog to become a public nuisance or cause unsanitary conditions.

X. Do not be unkind to your dog by overfeeding him so that he becomes lazy, unwatchful, clumsy, and ill.

IN PRAISE OF THE WORD 'BITCH'

The dog in ancient times and even near to our own day was considered low and worthless. What the dog thot of humans who were steeped in cruelty and who seldom practiced the trait of kindness or felt a sympathetic consideration for others, we can not know.

If there was a balance in the scale of worthiness, it leaned to the side of the canine. The dog served his master, guarded his property and protected his children; yet he was mistreated and abused; kicked and scuffed; his bed in the gutter; never fed—his meals out of the swill barrel.

The female dog, in the periodic course which comes to her sex in all species of life, (tho to her but two times in the year), accepts romance where she first finds it and with full modesty, without regard to place or eye of humans. In these matters nature is no prude. The female dog is as virtuous as any of her sex in any species of the animal kingdom.

And so, when one person out of anger and a mean heart, wishes to wound the feelings of another, he calls him the son of a bitch, that is, the offspring of a female dog, intending with this phrase to insult him and his mother with an insult no later apology can lessen.

We must not lose a good and correct word out of our language because of the ignobleness of men's minds and the malice of their tongues. If there be any change, let it be in the human mouth and mind thru disinfecting.

Bitch is a word to be used at all times when reference is to the female dog just as we speak the similar terms of cow, hen, mare and ewe; and to be used publicly and privately alike. To avoid such use is to confess helplessness against our own foulness of thot. Bitch is a word as fit, as logical for the speech of children and of men and women, as any other word, even in a book of holy wisdom.

(NOTE—A Dog's Prayer, with the possible exception of Senator Vest's Tribute, is the most quoted, most often reprinted item on the dog. The Prayer has appeared in numerous foreign languages.)

A Dog's Prayer for His Master

O LORD OF HUMANS, make my master faithful to his fellowmen as I am to him. Grant that he may be devoted to his friends and family as I am to him.

MAY HE BE openfaced and undeceptive as I am; may he be true to trust reposed in him as I am to his.

GIVE HIM a face cheerful like unto my wagging tail. Give him a spirit of gratitude like unto my licking tongue.

FILL HIM WITH patience like unto mine that awaits his footsteps uncomplainingly for hours. Fill him with my watchfulness, my courage, and my readiness to sacrifice comfort or life itself.

KEEP HIM always young in heart and crowded with the spirit of play, even as I.

MAKE HIM as good man as I am dog. Make him worthy of me, his dog.

WHITE WONDER. SHERBOURNE QUEEN.

STILL 'MAN'S BEST FRIEND'

Bringing up a puppy to doghood is an achievement and also a practical course in teaching. One becomes a master of animal psychology and an expert in pedagogy. Even the bachelor and spinster dog owners go thru the similar duties of a parent.

But the work and the worry, the cleaning up after the puppy, the reprimands and the disappointments—all are worthwhile and are well repaid by the dog as he develops into an appreciative, loyal, obedient, faithful member of the household.

A little soft warm bundle of fur which came into your home greatly frightened, biologically one of the beasts of the field, has almost bridged the wide gap between the human race and the animal kingdom. He has come out of the fields and forests of his ancestors to live by your side in the midst of modern civilization; and he makes the adjustment splendidly.

There is no other instance of such great progress from one stage to another as that of the dog, which adjusts himself to all the needs and desires of man. He comes from savagery to civilization within the short period of twelve months and indeed represents man's greatest achievement over the animal kingdom.

Give that four-footed member of your family the consideration and care to which you are obligated; and when in old age he moves slowly, his eyes water, and he dreams of puppyhood days, his passing on will be that of a loved and lovable member of the family whose soul never knew dishonesty and deceit.—

THE MIRACLE OF MATING AND BIRTH IS BEING CLIMAXED

The work of dog breeding has these progressive steps—choice of parents, the mating, the period of in whelp or pregnancy of the dam or bitch, the whelping of the litter of puppies, nursing and care of puppies for the first eight weeks, care, development and supervision of the puppies after eight weeks.

But the most interesting, most fascinating of the six steps is the delivery or whelping of the puppies out of the mother's womb. Something new comes into the world of conscious being; life appears for the first time to the outside world; the miracle of mating and birth is being climaxed. The spark of being bursts into the full flame of life—and the dog breeder therefore, if he be a true devotee of the sport of breeding, never fails to enjoy anew each time the thrill of ushering a new litter into the world of dogs and humans.—

THE SIXTEEN PRINCIPLES OF DOG PEDAGOGY

1. All dog training must be founded upon "educating" the dog, that is, first drawing out of him and developing his instincts, and secondly, accidental and acquired abilities.

2. Situations and contacts must be interpreted entirely from the dog's, not the human's reactions and abilities.

3. The dog is not to be fooled. He has a sense of humiliation and of pride. If he has been taught to do a certain act, do not give him the command and then trifle with him. At all times let him see what you are doing.

4. Success must be at the completion of an act of training. The dog is to understand that at the end a certain thing will take place; for instance, if he is trailing, he must find the object trailed. Always he is to understand that when you say certain things, he is to do certain things; there must not be any break in this seeming cause and effect.

5. Commands should be given consistently in the same words and with the same tone of voice and speed of speaking.

6. Do not punish the dog for failures to obey unless you are certain that he understood fully what you commanded.

7. Give the dog a moment's time for carrying out your command. To demand instant obedience often is to confuse the dog.

8. Anticipate the dog's actions. Think ahead of him. Give your command not to step over a boundary line before he reaches the line.

9. If the dog does one step wrongly, do not repeat this step but begin again at the beginning for the dog must be taught to consider only successful acts in their entirety.

10. The dog has a single-track mind. Teach one specific thing at a time. This does not mean that a training period can not include a half-dozen different tasks.

11. Reward should follow after every act done properly. Punishment should follow after every disobedience or failure.

12. Reward or punishment should follow quickly after the act. To punish a dog at any time other than instantly after the wrong act, is cruelty rather than a part of training, for the dog, particularly a puppy, does not connect the punishment with the act.

13. Instruction should not be too long, as a dog, especially one under

eight months, tires easily. An hour twice daily is sufficient length of time for special training work.

14. Try to locate each activity and command at or near the same location. If you call "brush," it should be at or near the place you groom the dog. This rule is based upon the law of association of ideas.

15. Do not lose your temper while training the dog. If you do, he loses some of his respect for you.

16. Have patience. The dog is not a human being. He probably is more successful as a dog than you are as a human being. His pleading liquid eyes and his wagging tail tell that he wants to do what you would have him do but that you are not as intelligent as he, else you would tell him in his language what you wish to say to him.

THE DOG AS A WORD STUDY IN INTERNATIONAL ORTHOGRAPHY

The word dog in other languages is an interesting study of orthografy. In Chinese—kou. In Danish, German and Norwegian—hund. In French—chien. In Hebrew—keleb. In Irish (Gaelic)—cu. In Italian—cane (from Latin canis). In Japanese—inu. In Belgian, hond.

In Dutch—hond. In Polish—pies. In Russian—sobaka. In Spanish—perro. In Swedish—hundar. In Czech—pes. In Hungarian—kutya. In Welsh—ki (note similiarity to Gaelic cu). In Mexican—perro; in Spain—perros.

In Polish—pies. In Lithuanian—suo.

Ch. Woodcote Pride.

BULL TERRIER. DALMATIAN.

WHY PEOPLE OWN DOGS

Someone wrote to me and suggested that I write on why people own dogs. I said, "Sure—it's a good subject." Now that I am writing on it, I have difficulty in keeping the keys of the typewriter clicking along smoothly.

Approximately 18,000,000 people in America own dogs. Now this hardly could be the situation if there were not one or more reasons why they own these dogs—and the reasons must be good ones. Very well, you as a dog owner are reading this installment of Dog TALKS. Just why do you own a dog?

I would classify the reasons into three general groups: 1. Usefulness. 2. Companionship. 3. Personal vanity.

There is little need of explaining No. 1. No history can tell us just when man and dog became a team—when the dog as a wild animal, slipped over the boundary line and made concessions in order to be with or near mankind.

That first association was based upon the aid the dog gave the caveman in hunting for food. It was a mutual enterprise, because the dog received parts of the prey as his share, and, of course, the thrill of the chase and the kill appealed to the dog as it did and still does. I often conclude that the enthusiasm of the dog in the hunting scene is mostly in the sport of the chase and rather minor in the actual killing and eating of the game. He is, first of all, a sportsman.

In time, as man tended to become less nomadic and acquire his food and livelihood from herds of sheep and cattle, the dog took up the duties of guarding the animals both night and day against other animals of prey and against thieves. The dog acquired a sense of property indentification and became accustomed to guarding his master's goods and family.

This sense of property—of "what's the master's is the master himself" —has continued without a break, and today the duty as watch dog remains as a basic and perhaps first purpose of the dog.

The dog, winning the label of "man's best friend" has added to his claims of usefulness such work as guide for the blind; as sentry, patrol, and messenger on the battlefield; as rescuer of humans from drowning; as announcer of fires and other dangers; as sled dog and bearer of packs in the snowlands; and if you wish, you may add—as cinema star in Hollywood.

THE SECOND BASIC reason why folks own dogs is also one of

benefit to the human and indirectly also has a background of human selfishness. It is for companionship.

I need not dwell greatly on this for any dog owner knows well what company a dog can be, how much more interesting the hours are if your dog is around—playing, exploring, and even making himself a pleasing nuisance.

How many thousands, or shall I say millions, of persons returning to their homes after the day's work, would find the return a somber, lonely thing, if there were not a dog—eager, devoted sincere, and without deceit, awaiting their very first footsteps?

THE THIRD BASIC reason for dog ownership I have given as personal vanity. This includes various backgrounds.

A few persons do own dogs in order to counteract their own inferiority complexes, inasmuch as to the dog, his master is a mighty person—the most important personage in the world.

Others have dogs because it's the fashion. They buy the breed that is the canine vogue (or they occasionally do just the opposite—they buy a rare breed for their own distinction). As a rule, their dogs are to be pitied for the sense of obligation for care, control, and training too often does not exist in the owner.

And, of course, there is milady who wants something novel to match her hair; a blue poodle or an apricot afghan or a blonde cocker is just the thing. But alas and alack, if milady dyes her hair, she must change the breed!—DOG TALKS (author's syndicated newspaper feature).

'My good man, have you ever heard of the SPCA?'

TRUE TALES OF BRAVE DOGS

The Chained Tragedy

Not far from where I live, the folks had a German shepherd dog—you'd term him a police dog. When I would take my dog (a smooth foxterrier) out for his evening exercise, the two never failed to pass the time of the day with the usual snarls and grunts, each suspicious of the other and each trying to bluff the other. Dogs, you know, are clever poseurs!

The other day my dog ran by with his usual challenge; but no shepherd responded. He came closer and even went into the yard, still there wasn't a challenge—and there never will be another.

My neighbor's house on Walnut Ave. had caught on fire in the basement. The shepherd dog barked and barked; the family were on the third floor and at last aroused by the howling, opened the door only to have a blast of smoke and gas sweep the room.

They had only a minute's time to rush down the stairway to safety as the flames quickly shut off every means of escape. In a few moments the fire had gutted the building.

As the fire department outened the last of the flames, the little boy cried out: "Where's Prince?" The firemen found him—in the basement, his body black and charred, tied to a chain.

He saved the lives of those he loved and gave his own life, trapped and helpless, a chain holding him to his death amid the stifling fumes, but the last sound from his swelling, burning, paining throat was a faint bark to warn the family of danger.

This hero of a dog who gave his life, was a needless sacrifice, due to the thotlessness of those he loved. He saved others; himself he could not save.

If you love your dog, give him the run of the house. Some day he may need to save your lives and his own from fire.—Date 1931, in Chicago.

IT'S THE WAY OF A DOG

On Nov. 13, 1954 the will of Mrs. Josephine Zuzak in Paterson, N. J., was announced. She left $1,000 for the care of her 9-yr-old mongrel Sandy. Some folks tittered over the idea of leaving money for the care of a dog.

Eleven days later, on Nov. 24, Sandy was dead. He had refused to eat or drink since his mistress' death. The official report read: "Died of a broken heart."

Bobbie Trots 2,600 Miles Back to His Home

About the year 1930 a collie dog by the name of Bobbie passed away. To me Bobbie is one of the great dog heroes of all time and worthy of occupying a niche in the canine hall of fame along with Barry, Rin Tin Tin, Gelert, Greyfriar's Bobby, and others.

His story is almost beyond belief but here truth is stranger than fiction, for as I shall relate Bobbie's wonderful achievement was checked up later and found to be one hundred percent true.

In the autumn of 1923, G. F. Brazier of Silverton, Oregon, stept into his auto and Bobbie, just a young dog, born and raised there and never before out of the town, leaped in with Mr. Brazier and family, and they started on a tour eastward across the country.

On their return trip they stopt for a moment at Logansport, Ind., to take on gas. Bobbie must have spied a cat around the corner; at any rate, when Mr. Brazier was ready to go, Bobbie couldn't be found, even after a search. So reluctantly they resumed their trip, which ended in the Oregon home, 2,600 miles away by road travel.

The Brazier family settled down again to routine living. Now and then the young boy asked for Bobbie but the father explained that Bobbie had been lost or had died far across the Rockies, the Dakota plains, the prairies, the Mississippi river and in the Midwest near Ohio and Pennsylvania.

One evening, about five months after their return, the family was eating supper as dusk was deepening into darkness. The little boy thot he heard a scratching at the door but no one paid any attention. The second time he heard it and his father told him to be still. But a minute later everyone at the table heard a low, familiar whining outside the door.

They rushed from the table to the door, opened it, and there, caked with mud and filth, his body almost raw and bare of hair, his bones almost piercing thru the skin, his toe nails worn into the bleeding flesh, stood Bobbie.

He wagged his tail feebly, and as they spoke to him and he heard the voices he had loved, he fell to the floor in his weakness, overcome with joy.

He had found his way home over river and field, thru woods, cities and traffic, 2,600 miles, to those whom he loved and for whom he would give his life, and without whom he considered his own life not worth living.

The story of his feat was disbelieved. A special expedition set out from Logansport, Ind., and at last the entire route was pieced together as here and there a garage man, a station agent, a bus driver, or a farmer at the cross roads would say "Yes, in such and such a month, such and such dog passed here and I gave him something to eat."

It was Bobbie. And now, passed away into dog heaven, he holds the world's record for a dog finding his way home.

ORIGINAL BULL AND TERRIER CROSS.

THE OLD DOG (OR 'GOODBYE TO DUCHESS')

The canine race parallels the human race in many phases—anatomy, internal organs, digestive reactions, mental responses.

Likewise, there is as much individuality among dogs as among humans. No two dogs are alike. Each has its own distinguishing habits, traits, reactions, responsiveness to commands. Consequently the wise exception must be made at all times and each dog considered as a unit of its own.

THE 7 TO 1 FORMULA

This parallel is carried over into old age. We can illustrate by telling of a cocker spaniel bitch in our home. Our titian-tressed wife christened her Duchess Miss Judy and the little golden blonde spaniel ever lived up to her title in demeanor, pretense and wilful disobedience. She and her mistress on parade on Michigan Boulevard or on Drexel Boulevard, in Chicago, where we lived, were a colorful, happy pair.

She came to us as a five-months puppy, with a family background of outdoor life, unheated kennels, and primal animal stamina. She soon owned us and was part and parcel of our lives for more than thirteen years. She died not quite 98 years old, if we carry on with a human parallel of seven to one, a formula originated by the writer.

The loss of eyesight in one eye at the age of ten slowed her up; it was due to a severe blow on the opposite side of the head we surmised. A very bad case of pyorrhea plagued her during the last four years of her life, it necessitated almost all of her teeth being extracted.

THE TELL-TALE STAIRWAY

A slowing down due to old age was not plainly noticeable until about twelve when she did not bound up and down the stairway as lightly. Soon she went up step by step—slowly, deliberately and at an angle.

Perhaps we do not make enuf allowance in our consideration of the short-legged breeds such as scotties, dachs, pekes and cockers in going up a stairway, each of whose steps is as high as the dog. It is equivalent to the average human going up a stairway whose treads are five feet high.

APPETITE LAUGHED AT THE YEARS

By the age of thirteen, she was carried up the stairway frequently, and as far as we could observe—to her delite.

Her dislike of rainy weather and wet ground increased.

Her bark was not as lusty, not as full of volume; the pitch went up. But her appetite continued unabated. Her coat took on a luster of oil which made it nigh perfect.

NO BOUNCE—ALAS, OLD AGE!

But during the last three months of her life, she took on senility rapidly, completely. She slept much, heard few sounds (she had become deaf over a period of the last twelve months), did not recognize old acquaintances readily. Her legs were stiff and their was no bounce in her step.

THE HABIT PATTERN OF INSTINCT

During the last thirty days of her life, there was only a body remaining. She became a chattering octogenarian, without keen canine intelligence. The mind was gone altho occasionally she returned to her former gaiety and habits for a brief interval, as a relic of instinct, of force of habit, an automatic reaction like that which enables a boxer to move and punch after his mind has blanked out.

She lost her sense of direction altho her nose still kept some sensitiveness. But to get thru a door, she would stand in a corner of the room, far from the door, and paw furiously against the wall; the years of custom were urging her to scratch somewhere, a necessity she recalled vaguely in getting thru a door

THE MEMORY PICTURE OF FRISKY

The decline in faculties was pathetic, yet we still saw her in our memory's mind as a gay, care-free, lively, lusty little dog, taking part in everything we did and even trying, vainly of course, and out of vanity, to learn what we were talking about.

The day before we had her put to sleep, she recognized only one member of the family, our wife, who of course had been her constant companion thru the years, on a thousand auto journies, in living room and bedroom alike—almost twenty-four hours of every day.

THE INEVITABLE STILL CAUSED US TO SHUDDER

Yet it was not easy to give her the lethal injection. To blot out a living thing entirely and forever, is not a light matter. But we knew bitterly that there was no hope of change in the immediate or far future. Nature was running its course, as it will do with you and us. The final act only brot a slightly earlier ending to a physical thing of life out of which the soul, mind, and personality had fled

And along those Elysian trails, where rabbits uncatchable bound out of every bush and hedge, where juicy golden bones are available instantly upon a bark—good hunting and happy living, Dutchess Miss Judy, a bundle of buff golden cocker beauty that lived as happy a life on earth as any dog could have lived

DOGS CAN BE TUFFIES

The English press reports that a dog named Rex had been given up as dead on account of being buried in the debris of his master's home, that of W. J. Humphries, Birmingham, Eng., when an enemy bomb struck the house.

Six weeks later, as reported in the English Weekly Dog World: "Mr. Humphries returned to the house to salvage what he could of his goods, and while searching among the wreckage, heard a whimper. With his bare hands Mr. Humphries began to dig and he found Rex lying helpless under the twisted remains of a bed. Rex could not stand for three days, but with careful attention he is recovering. It is hoped that he will pull thru after his terrible experience."

The Editor has been criticized severely for stating in his various books that many dog owners are cruel to their dogs thru the mistaken kindness of overfeeding them. Few dogs die of starvation; most dogs die indirectly thru the contrary, being overfed and consequently acquiring digestive ills, which in turn lead on to vital illness.

ONE MEAL PER DAY

We have advocated only one meal a day for any dog over twelve months of age except that the very large breeds should not be cut down to one meal until after the age of twenty months. Further, the average period of time required for food to pass entirely thru the digestive system of the dog is 16 to 17 hours.

WORLD'S RECORD FOR SURVIVAL

About twelve years ago we reported in DW the story of a collie in Connecticut, whose leg had been caught in a trap in the woods and in the dead of winter. The plight of the collie was discovered and the dog still alive, was nursed back to health altho the one front leg had to be partially amputated. And—as ascertained—the dog had been held in the trap for 56 days, exposed to the snows and storms of winter.—

COULDN'T TALK

Flash—the press in early April of this year told of a stowaway dog discovered after 21 days out at sea, exhausted, locked in the hold of the ship. The dog had trotted aboard the ship at the African port, was imprisoned in the hold, and went without food and water for three weeks.

The Animal Rescue League of Boston took care of the dog upon arrival and sought to restore it to health.

THE STRONG EAT "NOT OFTEN"

Stanley Benson, Loda, Ill., cockers, calls our attention to Peter Freuchen's book Arctic Adventure, particularly the portion concerning feeding, as follows:

"Dogs are fed mostly on walrus hide cut into large chunks just possible for them to swallow. On sledge trips we feed our dogs every second day, and at home, during the winter when they are doing no work, every third day. Later on when it is warmer, they require less food, and in summer, when they are tethered along a brook or at some pond, they need to be fed no oftener than once a week

"The dogs realize that when they are at last let to food, they must store up for a long interval. They are never as good on trips the days after they have been fed as when they are expecting food at night and are hungry."

NATURE AND STAMINA ARE GOOD NURSES

Our friend S. B. emphasizes in the following, a point we have made numerous times, namely that we are inclined to make too much fuss over the bitch when she is whelping.

"Recently the temperature dropped during the night from around 30 to about zero. At the time we had two cocker bitches with puppies under three weeks old, kept in unheated quarters. Each was well bedded down in boxes filled with fresh straw.

"When I discovered how cold it had turned, I went out the next morning half expecting to find the little puppies frozen to death. However, they were all well and apparently comfortable and I am therefore wondering how cold it would have to get to endanger puppies."

INJURED DOG IN BLIZZARD

Footnote: We are in receipt of a clipping from the Wisconsin State Journal telling of a collie caught by the foot in a twisted wire fence. The dog was held there in the open without food for 24 days.

During this time there was a blizzard which ran the thermometer down to 10 below zero on two successive nights.

She had lost 25 lbs.; her foot was a mass of frozen blood; hazel brush within reach of the dog was stripped and gnawed by her, both in pain and hunger. The news item concluded: "Ginger is rapidly gaining her weight back."—

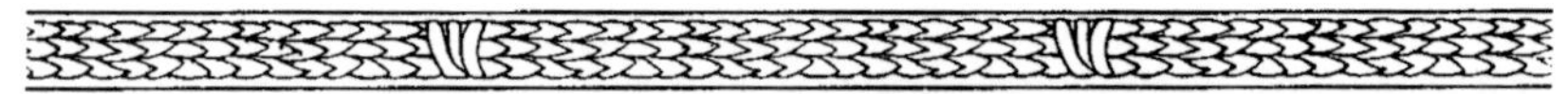

Why the World Likes Dogs

THE MOST UNSELFISH living thing in the world is your dog. If you are in danger, your dog needs only to hear your cry of distress to rush to your aid, without thot of his own life, fearless of guns and enemies.

THE MOST PATIENT thing in the world is your dog, waiting for hours at the door to hear the sound of your footsteps, never complaining however late you may be.

THE MOST GRATEFUL thing in the world is your dog. Whatever you give him, whatever you do for him, he never is guilty of ingratitude. A pat of the hand, a soft-spoken word from you are golden pay. To him you are the most powerful personage in the world and beyond censure; you are your dog's god; you can do no wrong.

THE MOST FRIENDLY thing in the world is your dog. Of all the animal kingdom, he alone serves man without whip, without compulsion, glad to be by the side of his master wherever he may be, whatever he may do, and sad in heart when his master is away.

THE MOST FORGIVING thing in the world is your dog. The one virtue most humans lack is that of forgiveness. But your dog carries no grudge and no spite. Punish him even undeservedly, and he comes to you, nudges his moist nose against your hand, looks up at you with pleading eyes,and wags his tail hesitatingly as tho to say, "Oh, come on, let's be pals again."

THE MOST LOYAL thing in the world is your dog. Whether you come home from Congress or from jail, whether you have lost your fortune or made a million, whether you return dressed in fashion's splendor or in wretched rags, whether you have been hailed hero or condemned as criminal, your dog is waiting for you with a welcoming bark of delight, a wagging tail and a heart that knows no guile.

The world likes dogs because dogs are nearest to moral perfection of all living things.

No Room in Heaven for Dogs

(AN ANSWER BY THE EDITOR OF DOG WORLD TO A LETTER FROM A 12-YEAR OLD SCHOOL BOY)

I am sorry that your Sunday School teacher told you 'there is no room in heaven for dogs." I can understand that this statement has disturbed you considerably.

Heaven is a big place because heaven is God and God stretches from the sun to the moon, to the stars, and back to earth.

Heaven must be a big place to hold all the good people who have died in the many years since the world began. As angels have wings, heaven must give them plenty of space in which to spread these wings and fly from one shifting cloud to another.

The millions upon millions of folks who have owned dogs and gone on to their heavenly home, surely would feel lonely without their dogs. And as there is no loneliness in heaven, God has made provision for man's best friend to dwell therein. We are certain of this, for it was God who named the dog by spelling His own name backwards.

Yes, heaven is a big place, with lots of shady spots, long lanes banked with flowers, fountains bubbling up out of the earth, good little rabbits munching on golden carrots, and by their side good dogs, big and little, dozing in the pure sunshine of celestial spaces.

It would be surprisingly strange, were there no dogs in heaven, for I believe that Christ had a little dog which followed him back and forth from Nazareth to Judea, thru the streets of Jerusalem, and cuddled trustingly in the boat when He crossed the stormy sea of Galilee.

It seems to me I can see, on that tragic afternoon on Calvary, as Christ cried out "Why hast Thou forsaken me?", a little dog whining vainly at the foot of the cross to lick His bleeding hands. I believe that today this same little dog can be no other place than in heaven with Christ his master, lying contentedly at the foot of the throne of God.

I am sorry indeed that someone gave you the misinformation that "there is no room in heaven for dogs."

The Dog and Words

The inability of a dog to understand words as words, brings a touch of pathos. Often we have put on our hat and coat while the dogs leap about joyously and optimistically. Of course, they expect to go with us—no doubt about it in their minds.

There was no manner of word, gesture or action, by which we could tell them we would be away for only 30 minutes; that they should not worry; that this was not a long journey.

It is impossible to convey this idea to the dog's mind because of the lack of words which the dog can understand as expression of an idea. The dog can talk and at both ends but words fail him—he can not use an alfabet or read a dictionary.

The Dog Does Not Suffer by Comparison

I think it is hardly fair to refer to animals as the lower or dumb creation. Judged as animals, perhaps they live up to their standards of perfection better than we live up to our human standards.

Animals don't carry gossip or bear false witness; they don't rob banks; they don't sneak through traffic signals; they don't get drunk; they don't amass great wealth for their own selfish uses; and when they have eaten enough, they quit eating and lie down and sleep in the sunshine, an example all of us humans well might follow.

The dog is the only animal that talks at both ends. He uses his voice and his tail. There is nothing in this world more expressive than a dog's tail except perhaps a woman's smile.

Dog (and pet) cemetery at Scarsdale, N. Y. All is silent—not a bark is heard; yet the dog owner coming back can hear clearly again in memory the bark of his dog, and see the wagging tail, the bounding leap of joy. Alas, that the span of a dog's life should be so distressingly brief in comparison to his owner's!

'Going to the Dogs' is Nice Trip in Present Day and Age

At one of the preliminary gatherings for the dog show, it was my good fortune to encounter an old friend, Will Judy, who would be among the first to insist that 'going to the dogs' is a sure route to prosperity.

Will is publisher of 'Dog World,' whose offices are here in Chicago. He acquired the magazine some 30 years ago as something to keep his print-shop busy.

Today the publication, a Chicago product, is not only one of the largest and most authoritative in its field, but Judy himself is recognized as one of the world's outstanding dog experts. He is so prominent in this field that he has participated in shows in no less than 21 foreign nations.

At the moment he is home from a trip to India, where he officiated at four shows. I was interested in knowing whether judging in India, for instance, was any different than at some show like the one starting to-morrow. He replied:

'No, not a great deal. If you know 'em in one country, you can judge anywhere. Standards are the same. So far as spectators are concerned, the shows in India drew the same kind of people we attract here, aside from the fact that a certain percentage wear native costume.'

Judging show dogs is highly-specialized art. Each breed has its own standards, which differ greatly. When you figure that there are 112 recognized breeds, you can see what a field this has become.

Most judges are specialists in one breed or another. According to Judy, only 52 persons are certified as allbreed judges. Will, whose dog travels have taken him from Iceland to Africa, says it isn't as complicated as it sounds. He explains:

'Breeds are virtually the same everywhere. No matter where you judge, you'll find few native breds. In India, I encountered the Tibetan mastiff, which is as big as a St Bernard and generally regarded as the most vicious of all dogs. Maybe that's why you seldom see them.'

Judy had a few other items which indicate the extent of dog interest. Said he:

'In the United States there are 1,892 small animal hospitals. Most of their practice is with dogs. You might also get an idea of what a big business the dog business is when you realize that aside from soups, the largest selling canned-goods item is dog food.'

WE ARE VICARS OF GOD

The Almighty created humans with the possibilities lurking within themselves of becoming godlike, approaching even to the Creator himself.

All other living things of the animal kingdom are termed the dumb creation or the lower animals. This term of inferiority is man-made and may not be in accord with the Creator's design of importance.

In primeval days the animals of the field and forest were on more nearly equal terms with the human animals. In this present age, with its myrials of inventions and machines, man has adjusted himself but the lower animals still retain mostly the capabilities of the primeval days, not having developed a language and a set of fingers and thumbs.

Therefore, the obligation is upon us to do for these living things that which they cannot do for themselves—to avoid unnecessary pain and suffering, to have opportunity to live their lives naturally and rear their young safely, and to have the means of fulfilling their varying purposes in the plan of creation.

Surely we are only being appreciative of our status in the celestial scheme of things when we show consideration to all other living things and thereby, as it were, stand in the stead of the Creator.

It is for man, the allegedly superior animal, to show this superiority in kindness rather than force, in sympathetic understanding rather than brutal disregard.

We are vicars of God in this respect. Truly there is no surer way for the human soul to climb the heights than to have a constant, kindly regard for those considered as not having a soul or at best, an inferior one.—

SOME OF THE BEST.

Mrs. Adlam, owner of a noted kennel of Bull Terriers, which is one of the best in the world, with Ch. "Brendon Gold Standard" and Ch. "Brendon Beryl" with "Boomerang". Notice the ears and heads.

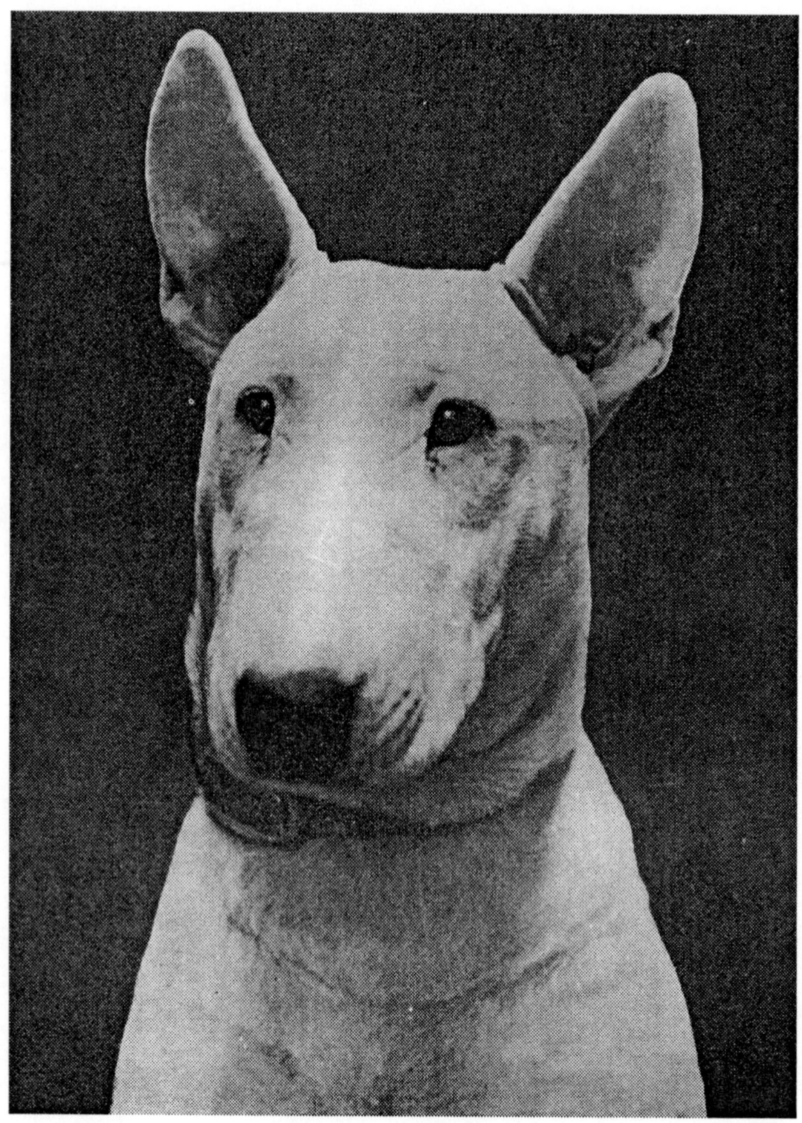

CH. "MITSU DANNEBROG".
Here we have the typical head of the Bull Terrier of 1934. The dog was bred by Major Mitford Brice. The reader's attention is drawn to the head of "Old Dutch" opposite.

Suggested FBI for Dog Owners

As time goes by, I am more and more convinced that the greatest need in the dog world today is the intensified education of the dog owner not only in technical matters of dog care but also in a sense of personal responsibility for the welfare of the dog he owns.

This is especially true of the dog owner whose dog must find his kennel in the house or apartment for virtually such a dog is a prisoner within its walls. He can not come and go as he pleases; a closed door makes a room a jailhouse for him. Hence the ethical obligation of the owner to supervise and provide for the dog's comfort and welfare.

I give these personal interrogatories as a 'third degree' for the dog owner, knowing he will not mind my 'direct' approach.

---

1. Did you apologize to Neighbor Smith when your dog dug up his tulip bulbs last spring?

2. Didn't you complain to the veterinarian about his charge although the services were given to clear up a skin condition which developed because you neglected to stop it in its earliest stages?

3. Will you cease slipping tidbits to your dog under the table when the family is eating?

4. Evidence has been presented against you that you whipped your dog for soiling in the house; that this happened during the night on which you neglected to take him out for his usual run because of the chill, rainy weather. Guilty or not guilty?

5. Your dog jumped up playfully on Mr Abarbanell last week. It was a rainy day as you may recall. His overcoat was badly soiled.
Have you offered to pay the cleaner's bill?

6. Your dog barked incessantly last night to neighborhood's annoyance while you were away until late. What are you going to do to avoid a recurrence of this?

7. You know how much the Kittrell family fear germs; you know they haven't been back to visit your home since last year. You know that you did not reprimand your dog when he licked the faces of the small Kittrell children. Who is to be blamed for this lost friendship?

8. The blanket on which your dog Spot sleeps has a strong odor. When did you launder it last?

9. You promised not to lose your temper over Spot. But yesterday you flew in a rage when you came upon him chewing a sock of yours you had carelessly left lying on the floor. If your dog could talk, what would be his opinion of you in a few well-chosen canine comments?—

The Dog Issues 'His' Ten Commandments

In another article I set forth Ten Commandments for the Dog Owner—basic duties he must perform in behalf of his dog. Now I am going to give Ten Commandments which the dog likely would issue, could he talk or write.

The publishing field is flooded with books and other literature on dogs. But my observation is that they almost all are based too greatly on what the author thinks the dog thinks. The true treatment of subject matter should be to seek to ascertain what the dog thinks and how he looks at human and his own problems.

I am almost nauseated by the writers (and some dog owners too) who attribute human virtues, abilities, and thinking processes to the dog. It is more logical and sensible to keep the dog as a dog than to try to change him into a second-rate human. Rather let us seek to improve him as a dog, develop his abilities to the fullest extent as a dog and according to nature's mould. I prefer dogs 100 percent dog to dogs 80 percent human.

Here are ten commandments which I think the wise dog would impose upon his master, the controller of his welfare, the dictator of comfort, health and life itself.

---

1. Be sure you know more than I do before you attempt to teach and train me.
2. Look at my problems or any of your efforts to train me through my eyes and mind.
3. Don't become impatient with me until after you are certain I understand fully what you want me to do. Get your ideas across to me. Remember—I don't speak with words.
4. Don't lose your temper; it only makes you look weak and ridiculous to us dogs.
5. Make sure the water in my drinking pan is not stale, dust-filled, or unclean. Don't put anything in my drinking dish except clean, pure water.
6. I haven't hands for using brush and comb; so please groom me at least once every two days, else don't complain about K9 BO.
7. If I bark when I hear strange sounds, don't reprimand me too quickly. It is not easy for me to tell who is friendly and who is intent upon doing harm.
8. Give me a bit of notice when you approach me, especially if I am sleeping, or have my back turned.
9. On the street, keep tab on me, especially if I spy another dog across the street. Don't let me leave the curb.
10. Be proud of me as I am of you. And please, if I am ill, don't wait too long before you take me to my favorite veterinarian.

THE DOG IS STILL 'MAN'S BEST FRIEND'

'I would sooner have a good faithful dog than a giddy wife that does not understand,' writes a listener to my radio talks.

Are you lonely? Are friends few? Does life seem hollow and cheerless to you? Are there no voices, no loving hands to greet you at the close of day as you return home? Then, buy a dog!

Rudyard Kipling the English poet, wrote a wonderful poem about dogs entitled The Power of the Dog, from which I quote:

'Buy a pup and your money will buy
Love unflinching that cannot lie—
Perfect passion and worship, fed
By a kick in the ribs or a pat on the head.'

When friends have deserted you, look for sympathy to your dog, Pity him who knows not the love of a dog.

There are thousands upon thousands of lonely people in this city and in all other places. Is there just a room and a bed in it—four walls in some rooming house, awaiting you after a hard day's toil as at eventide your steps turn homeward? Buy a dog. Nothing can fill the four walls of a room with so much life and cheerfulness, as a dog.

Then, some one who cares, will be awaiting you. A joyous bark, a leap into the air, a scamper here and there will be your welcome.

All thru the day some one moved about sort of despondent and as the day drew to its close, began to loiter near the door or the front window. And almost to a minute of your usual arrival, he stationed himself where he could catch the first glimpse of you as you turned the corner.

That's your dog, my friends, the most loyal, devoted, sacrificing of all living things.

Your dog cares not for prosperity or hard times. The rise and fall of stocks on Wall Street mean nothing to him. You may have had a disastrous day in your business, you may be down-hearted, but your dog is there to greet you with an optimism and cheerfulness, a wagging tail and joyous yelp, which put you and all other humans to shame.

You may have gone bankrupt, your business may be ruined, your friends gone—that makes no difference to your dog. To him you are a god, still the greatest and best man on earth.

And tho your room rent is past due, your trousers baggy at the knee, shoes down at the heel, and you're out of a job, your dog cares not; you are still his only lord and master, and to him, the pat of your hand, the sound of your voice, mean more than your bank account—your lands and estates—and all the rest of the world and the people in it.—

A PLEASING KIND OF INSANITY

That otherwise good people should travel the detour of a hobby and become abnormally zealous therein, at times to the detriment of their calling, is well known; but perhaps, it is not too well known that in this regard, indeed the most temperamental and seemingly fanatical are the dog breeders, the exhibitors at dog shows; and in general, all dog fanciers. Age is immaterial; the neophytes are as temperamental and high-strung as the oldtimers.

They appear to be abnormal; they resent, criticism; they extol their own dogs as the most desirable of all. Each one seeks the mirage of perfection in physical type, knowing full well that the perfect canine never exists — and so they learn to their disillusionment in the show ring time after time; but such defeats do not dampen their ardor thru the years.

They carry on furiously and at times vociferously. They may even neglect their own money-making calling or permit it to suffer. They are strange folk; they argue with and against one another; they become mad competitors; yet in an instant, they shake hands, embrace each other and the losers congratulate the victor.

Indeed here is strange company! On the whole they are warmhearted people; the subject of their hobby is a living, understanding thing; they deal in life itself; their obsession is not with ordinary live stock but with an animal which is said to come nearest to man in mental capabilities — namely, the dog, 'man's best friend,' so-called.

Yet notwithstanding all these things, we consider the dog people as warm-hearted and likeable folks tainted with a pleasing kind of insanity. —

'She Should Have Children'

How often have we heard the remark spoken sneeringly—'It would be better if she had some children instead of dogs.'

As with most snarls of human tongue, the logic of this statement is weak. Most women do not have dogs because they prefer dogs to children. Most women who have dogs, love dogs. Some women who have dogs, can not have children; and the companionship of the dog helps to fill an aching void inwardly. Many women who have dogs, have children—and some of them, a lot of them. If the women who have dogs, didn't have them, therefore, are we to conclude they would have children?

To you who may be frustrated, in one way or another, may suffer from an inferiority complex, may be lonely in your daily existence, you who may need the companionship of a living thing which depends utterly on you for its comfort and welfare—get a dog, own a dog, be owned by a dog; and let the scorners and the sneering would mildew in their own petty sewer of the soul.

PETS AS PRIZES

An item in the news just before Easter Sunday attracted my attention, namely, that a hundred chicks had been confiscated in Chicago because they had been colored. The state of Illinois makes the selling of artificially colored day-old chicks an offense, and wisely so, as the coloring may bring on early death.

'BARBARISM' OF THE PUBLIC

The item illustrates that the enthusiasm of tradesmen and advertisers must be restrained now and then. Another practice which is utterly abhorrent to us is the sale of lizards and chameleons; not one out of ten survives as long as three day after being sold, and often barbarically worn on the lapel by some child or grown-up. And I shan't spend words in telling how many gold and tropical fish, how many baby turtles meet up with quick death after sale in the shops.

I come now to my particular province, the dog. And especially to the custom of giving puppies as prizes in contests or as the prize to the lucky winner of a raffle.

NOT 'SHELF' GOODS

The breeder of livestock, whatever the species—horse, cattle, swine, sheep, goats, dogs, is not a manufacturer; he does not run a factory. He is dealing in a product which has life, has mental reactions, and is sensitive to pain, and which requires daily care and attention. The proprietor of a shoe factory can close up shop for a week or a month; but not so the breeder of livestock; he must be 'on the job' each day. Animals require food, water, control and care daily.

CANNOT SPEAK FOR THEMSELVES

The puppy is a living, breathing thing, helpless, away from its mother, brothers and sisters. It cannot cry out in words for help; it must endure any suffering or cruelty imposed upon it. No home should have a dog, which does not want the puppy, or if wanting it, does not realize the endless care and attention day after day the dog requires and rightly so.

KENNELS NOT 'SALES CRAZY'

We hope the many kennels who do not rush into a sale when a prospect is at hand but who first inquire about the home, environment, and the care the prospect can give to the puppy, we hope they will increase in number and maintain this sales policy. We do not want more dogs so much as better dog care; and we want better dog owners too.

THE 'PERSONAL' ELEMENT

I certainly cannot approve of any activity which for the sake of a sale, or publicity and notoriety, includes a pet as a prize. It must be labeled a cruel practice and I trust that it will diminish steadily until it has gone entirely. Always there must be the personal contact of a willing, conscientious owner, fully aware of the demands a pet makes on his time, patience and sympathies.—

Pity the Sick Dog

What is ahead for the sick animal in the fields? We all have seen a bird perched solemly without motion for hours. Likely this bird is in the last stages of a disease which soon will drop it to the ground.

Just so with the old animal, the sick animal in the forest, and the dog that cannot protect itself against other dogs, that cannot go out and forage for its own food, where it must match cleverness and strength against that of its prey. Instead, it must lie quietly awaiting the end of life.

Pity the old dog, the sick dog, the crippled dog in the wilds!

FIRST IN DOGS ALSO

George Washington the father of our country, first in war, first in peace, and first in the hearts of his countrymen, was perhaps the first dog breeder also. He fancied foxhounds and loved nothing better than to follow the chase of B'rer Fox. His diary is replete with reference to scent and to game caught. We quote as follows:

"*1785 December 5—It being a scenting morning, I went out with hounds. Run at two different foxes. Caught neither.*

"*1786 January 23—Went out with two Mr. Hansons and Mr. Alexander when they set out on their return after breakfast with the dogs, just to try if we could touch on a fox as we went along the road. This we did, but the scent being cold and seeing no great prospect of making it out the dogs were taken off and the gentlemen went home.*"

"FAITHFUL BARKING GHOST"

"But in some canine Paradise
Your wraith, I know, rebukes the moon.
And quarters every plain and hill,
Seeking its master. As for me
This prayer at least the gods fulfill
That when I pass the flood and see
Old Charon by Stygian coast
Take toll of all the shades who land,
Your little, faithful barking ghost
May leap to lick my phantom hand!"

—St. John Lucas

All Days Now Are 'Dog Days'

To lead a dog's life has been a way of expressing misery. Charity gave the dog at least one day of pleasure in his life; hence, we have heard often the old saying: 'Every dog has his day.'

But times have changed and if we may judge from the widespread interest taken in dogs and their breeding, every day is dog's day and to lead a dog's life, has its attractions, especially if he has a pretty mistress, who feeds him bon bons and does not permit him to sleep on anything less comfortable than a feather pillow in one of the best rooms of the house.

Some say that the city is no place for a dog. Many do not believe this for in our cities, the dog is more popular than ever and as pet and companion, he finds a place in twice as many homes as he did only ten years ago.

We may ask what animal deserves this popularity more than the dog? He returns ful value in fidelity, amusement and companionship for all the attention and expense he demands.

Let the dog have his day. He comes to us as man's most complete victory over the wild beasts. Perhaps one of the chief reasons why we like him much is that he still retains some of his wild, ancestral qualities, much admired by a generation that to a great extent, never gets into the forests and the haunts of wild life. Let the dog have his day; he deserves it; he is the most valuable prize man has won from the conquest of the animal kingdom.

The Shame of the Human Race

One need only visit a dog pound or animal shelter to be imprest with the sad truth that the human race in many instances is unworthy of dogs and of other members of the animal kingdom.

Recently we visited an animal shelter in just a short distance from Dog World's office.

We saw about 60 dogs peering thru the cage bars. There would be a look of hope in the eyes, an ear went up, the body would stiffen into alert attention — perhaps a familiar voice would be heard, a familiar human scent sniffed. Then came the inevitable disappointment—'no, he's not the one. Will he never come? What has happened to him?' And the dog settled back into the corner of the cage, put its head on its paws, and pretended to be unconcerned.

Don't visit a dog pound unless you are prepared to come away sad-hearted and with your inner self greatly disturbed.

In the meanwhile we ourselves will do our utmost and we ask all other dog lovers also to do their utmost to put all dog pounds out of business—by keeping the streets free from strays and by demanding better dog owners as well as better dogs, by limiting dog ownership to good homes and to folks worthy of being worshipt by a dog.

Firecrackers and Your Dog

I can title this article 'Your Dog and the Fourth of July' but that limits the basic idea, namely that sounds such as exploding firecrackers, the shooting off of a gun, the blowout of a tire strangely throw great, intense fear into the dog and into most species of animal life, especially including birds of the air.

PIGEONS DREAD IT

All of us have observed in the city that when a sound suggesting booming, bursting, exploding is heard, pigeons which had been feeding or moving calmly, suddenly fly up en masse and settle at a distance. They may be city veterans but nevertheless this practice persists at all times.

I believe there is every reason to conclude that the dog, the pigeon and other animals suffer intense mental agony. The twitching of the body, the alert ear and eye, the general demeanor indicate inner emotion. Consequently my first basic point is that we humans cease our usual laughter and ridiculing attitude in these instances. It is a serious situation—to the animals.

THE SINGING DOGS

There is still mystery in the dog's ear. Most dogs burst into a shrill, high-pitched semi-howl, semi-moan, head held high, when certain sounds are heard; for instance, a bugle, high C on the piano, and even the distant whistle of a diesel engine. I doubt that there is actual pain being felt by the dog; in fact, I suspect the dog enjoys it in a negative way. I recall a pekingese who, when My Wild Irish Rose was played on the piano, would jump on the piano stool, and pour forth an accompaniment worthy of any Irish tenor.

NOT OUT OF COWARDICE

Whence comes this fear of gunfiring, etc? Gun shyness is a serious fault in dogs; many otherwise good dogs are discarded accordingly. It does not arise out of cowardice. Perhaps two of every five dogs are its victim. Dogs are born with it—and these are helpless against it. Perhaps thru the generations, in nature's strange way, animals have had forced into their subconsciousness that any sound suggestive of a firing gun, means death, destruction, injury—in time it developed into a hereditary fear.

BE UNDERSTANDING

So, when the firecracker are heard on or before the Fourth of July and your dog trembles, runs under the bed, or comes to you pleading for sympathy, give it to him. Let him have a secluded corner somewhere, perhaps in the basement, during Independence Day. That is the best solution for this strange emotion.

GOING UP FOR JUDGMENT.

Whilst in the olden days dogs travelled in boxes, baskets, and even sacks to the various shows and newspaper correspondents went to them in fear and trembling), to-day they go on their way in cars, as do these Bull Terriers, "Jerry" and "Peg of Judington", the property of Mrs. Phillips.

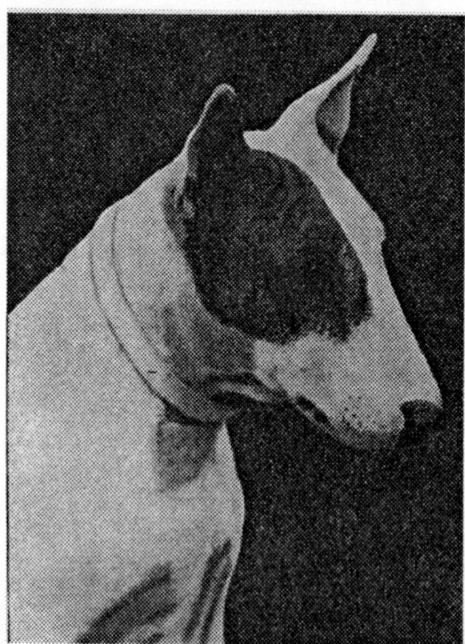

CH. "RHOMA".

Although Bull Terrier fanciers usually prefer a pure white dog, and much colour places it among the Staffordshires, a patch round the eye is allowed, though at one time this created ill-feeling—so much so that one noted dog is reported to have been poisoned by an irritated rival breeder.

CH. "BUTTERFLY WHITE BUD".

That the breed has not altered in recent years except to acquire greater quality may be noticed by comparing this champion of past days with dogs illustrated on other pages.

Lost Dog

Whatever the cause of the dog being away from its accustomed surroundings, away from the humans it regards as godlike and indispensable, the mental pain of the dog must be intense.

Who at one time or another has not seen a dog running strangely along the street, terror in its eyes, its movements indicating total bewilderment? If one tries to be kindly-disposed to the dog, to speak a soft word, to seek to pat the dog, it looks up with a ray of hope in its eyes, then as it realizes the person is not the one he seeks, the pang is sharper than ever and the dog rushes away, block after block, until—well, one wonders what will be the ending—death under grinding auto wheels, the remainder of the years in heartsick separation, or perhaps at last the happy ending—reunited with owners and family.

Let us be realistic. In most cases the lost dog is lost because of the owner's negligence, either accidental or habitual. Keep your dog under control, worry about him, don't permit him out of your sight—better still, in public places have him on lead.

The too friendly dog is a likely victim of being lost, of being enticed away. It is a fine line to draw especially for the dog, between being too friendly and being wisely aloof. Do not permit strangers to be too friendly with your dog. I know this is strange advice but I believe it is wise advice.

Dognappers are doing their work constantly—despicable humans who snatch a beloved dog away, then scan the papers for reward offer. Dog thieves of course always are to be feared—those who steal dogs for sale to unscrupulous dog shops, to other individuals, or to laboratories and medical school classes.

IF YOUR DOG IS LOST, SOUND THE NEWS EVERYWHERE. Scour the neighborhood promptly. Ask all neighbors whether they have seen your dog. Ads in newspapers of course are a necessity. Visit the dog pound and the local animal shelter. If school is in session, ask the principal to post a notice. Offer a reward to the children; they all become zealous detectives.

Do not give up hope. Dogs have returned or been returned six months to a year after disappearance.

I need not add that you should have an identification tag on the dog's collar—with phone number. Be able to describe your dog precisely for color, markings, habits, size, etc. Always mention call name of dog.

Best of all, alert yourself and family before the dog has disappeared. A trained dog, properly controlled, is less apt to stray away and less apt to permit itself to be picked up.

A TEAM.

There is nothing very much nicer than to see several dogs of the same variety standing side by side, and it is particularly interesting in a breed such as the Bull Terrier, for it allows comparison. Mrs. Yearsley's Bull Terriers are seen here.

The Faith of a Dog

I've hunted the woodland and hill,
And "pointed" the quail in my day,
I could freeze as rigid and still
As a stone—when scent blew my way.
I recall the time you lost me
And I "pointed" the long hours through—
Though the night was too dark to see,
You came, as I knew you would do.
You gave me a pat in the darkness
And your voice was roughened and gruff—
But I knew by that one caress
That you understood well enough.
I'm just a dog but I love you,
And though I am stiffened and old—
My heart is as brave and as true,
My spirit still dauntless and bold.
I know that my hunting is done
I no longer gambol and bark—
But this one desire I have won,
Your hand on my head—in the dark!

—MARGARET NICKERSON MARTIN
(blind poetess).

"Now I Have a Friend"

I had many friends in my lifetime—
Some who would borrow my very last dime;
I went thru life, earned what I spent
Paid what I owed, lost what I lent.
My partner in business ran off with my wife,
Then stole my child and ruined my life,
The big bank failed where I kept my dough,
My house burned down, I had no place to go.
They all quit me cold when I could not lend,
So I bought me a dog—now I have a friend.

—ANONYMOUS (but clever and "realistic"?)

Where to Bury a Dog

A subscriber of the Ontario Argus has written to the editor (Editor's note—Portland Oregonian, where this first appeared—about 1947) asking, "Where shall I bury my dog?"

We would say to the Ontario man that there are various places in which a dog may be buried.

We are thinking now of a setter, whose coat was flame in the sunshine, and who, so far as we are aware, never entertained a mean or an unworthy thought. This setter is buried beneath a cherry tree, under four feet of garden loam, and at its proper season the cherry strews petals on the green lawn of his grave.

Beneath a cherry tree, or an apple; or any flowering shrub is an excellent place to bury a good dog. Beneath such trees, such shrubs, he slept in the drowsy summer, or gnawed at a flavorous bone, or lifted head to challenge some strange intruder. These are good places, in life or in death.

Yet it is a small matter. For if the dog be well remembered, if sometimes he leaps through your dreams actual as in life, eyes kindling, laughing, begging, it matters not at all where that dog sleeps.

On a hill where the wind is unrebuked, and the trees are roaring, or beside a stream he knew in puppyhood, or somewhere in the flatness of a pasture land where most exhilarating cattle graze.

It is all one to the dog, and all one to you, and nothing is gained, and nothing lost—if memory lives. But there is one best place to bury a dog.

If you bury him in this spot, he will come to you when you call—come to you over the grim, dim frontiers of death, and down the well-remembered path, and to your side again. And though you call a dozen living dogs to heel, they shall not growl at him, nor resent his coming, for he belongs there. People may scoff at you, who see no lightest blade of grass bent by his footfall, who hear no whimper, people who may never really have had a dog.

Smile at them, for you shall know something that is hidden from them, and which is well worth the knowing. The one best place to bury a good dog is in the heart of his master.—*Ben Hur Lampman in his book* How Could I Be Forgetting? (Binfords & Mort).

An Outcast in Hell
(or the Dog Poisoner)

During a lull in the Stygian flames
  A group of shades were exchanging names,
And telling of places that they had been
  With bits of gossip and tales of sin.
A lonely shade who was standing by
  Approached to speak; but without reply
Each wrapped himself in his ghostly shawl!—
  Murderers, robbers and blackguards all—
With a whispered word and averted stare
  Vanished and left him standing there.
"*Who was he?*" *I asked as they turned and fled.*
  "*He poisoned his neighbor's dog,*" *they said.*

—AUTHOR NOT IDENTIFIED.

The Dog in the Library

(A prize winner in the National Dog Poetry Contest (year 1934) conducted by Dog World Magazine)

So good you never knew that he was there
  Until you came upon him in a nook
Beside the small gray woman as she searched
  The well-known shelves for some yet unread book.
He waited patiently as she would thumb
  The leaves, and when she sauntered on he went
Pad-footed at her side, a little dog
  Brown-patched, clean-white, devoted and content.
Perhaps this dalliance bored him but he gave
  No hint of tedium—no whimpered sound,
No tapping paws, no straining at the leash.
  Only, at times when girls and boys would bound
Into the quiet place his eager eyes
  Would follow them about the library,
And when swift choice they made and ran to play,
  He seemed to watch their going wistfully.

—ETHEL KING

THE STORY OF A GREAT LITERARY GEM

The world around, Senator Vest's Eulogy of the Dog is read and admired. Many varying stories have been written about the actual event, but a careful search of archives reveals the following, which the author assures is authentic.

On the front of the Old Courthouse in Warrensburg, Mo., a two-and-a-half story brick structure, no longer used, a bronze tablet bears this inscription:

> *"Within these walls on Sept. 23, 1870, Senator George Graham Vest delivered his famous eulogy on the dog. He died Aug. 14, 1904, and was buried in Bellefontaine Cemetery, St. Louis."*

Old Drum, a black and tan coonhound owned by Charles Burden, was enjoying one of his usual trailing jaunts thru the woods when a neighbor "Lon" Hornsby, redheaded and stubborn, shot Old Drum. However, it is to be noted that Hornsby, a reputable farmer and livestock rancher, had suffered the loss of more than 100 of his sheep during the few months previous.

On the evening of Oct. 28, 1869, Hornsby asked his companion, Richard Ferguson, to shoot the dog, as they detected Old Drum nearby in the twilight.

Burden filed a suit before the Justice of the Peace in Madison Township but the jury at the trial Nov. 25, 1869, failed to reach a decision and the case was set for retrial on the following Dec. 23.

Public feeling ran high on one side or the other and the second trial was well attended by farmers, cattle raisers and hunters of the area. Here Burden was awarded $25. Hornsby, his neighbor, appealed to Johnson County Court of Common Pleas. This new trial, in March, 1870, with two attorneys on each side, brought a verdict in favor of Hornsby.

Burden, in turn, asked for and won a new trial. This fourth trial became a public mass meeting with the crowds overflowing the capacity of the courthouse.

The wagering on the outcome of the trial was about even up to the point when George Graham Vest of Phillips and Vest of Sedalia, Mo., attorneys for Burden, arose for the final argument for their client—this on Sept. 23, 1870.

Vest spoke for only a few minutes. The jury came back promptly and returned the verdict in favor of Burden and Old Drum—for $50, twice the amount sued for originally.

Nine attorneys in all were connected with the case. One of them was David Nation, no other than the husband of the famous Carrie Nation. Elliott became judge of the Court of Common Pleas of Johnson County.

T. T. Crittenden later was elected governor of Missouri. Cockrell was a senator from that state for 30 years and afterward became a member of the Interstate Commerce Commission. John F. Phillips was appointed a commissioner of the Supreme Court of Mo. George Graham Vest was U. S. Senator from Mo. for 24 years.—Will Judy.

Senator Vest's Tribute to a Dog

THE TRIBUTE

THE BEST FRIEND a man has in the world may turn against him and become his enemy. His son or daughter that he has reared with loving care may prove ungrateful. Those who are nearest and dearest to us, those whom we trust with our happiness and our good name, may become traitors to their faith.

THE MONEY a man has he may lose. It flies away from him when he needs it most. A man's reputation may be sacrificed in a moment of ill-considered action. The people who are prone to fall on their knees to do us honor when success is with us, may be the first to throw stones of malice when failure settles its clouds upon our heads.

THE ONE absolutely unselfish friend that a man can have in this selfish world, the one that never deserts him, the one that never proves ungrateful or treacherous, is his dog.

A MAN'S DOG stands by him in prosperity and in poverty, in health and in sickness. He will sleep on the cold ground where the wintry winds blow and the snow drives fiercely if only he may be near his master's side. He will kiss the hand that has no food to offer, he will lick the sores and wounds that come in encounter with the roughness of the world. He guards the sleep of his pauper master as if he were a prince.

WHEN ALL other friends desert, he remains. When riches take wings and reputation falls to pieces, he is as constant in his love as the sun in its journey through the heavens.

IF MISFORTUNE drives the master forth an outcast in the world, friendless and homeless, the faithful dog asks no higher privilege than that of accompanying him to guard against danger, to fight against his enemies.

AND WHEN the last scene of all comes, and death takes the master in its embrace, and his body is laid away in the cold ground, no matter if all other friends pursue their way, there by the graveside will the noble dog be found, his head between his paws, his eyes sad, but open in alert watchfulness, faithful and true, even in death.

The Disadvantages of Being a Dog

Before a crowd of approximately three thousand townsfolk and visitors from all parts of America, the author gave the dedicatory address for the unveiling of the bronze statue to Old Drum as designed by the St. Louis sculptor Reno Gastaldi. The day was one of perfect autumnal weather in western Missouri. The date was 27 September 1958. A speakers' platform had been erected on the grounds of the new courthouse and from this rostrum, we gave our address. Notables from all walks of life were present. The actual unveiling was done by Honorable John Dalton, Attorney General of the State of Missouri. Our address on this occasion is given hereinafter. The press thruout the country gave the ceremony much mention.—WJ.

I am honored indeed to stand before you good people of Johnson County to do honor to a dog. Yet I find good reason for saying to you today on this memorable occasion that there should be a monument erected to the dog's owner Charles Burden inasmuch as his persistence even unto the fourth court trial in order to uphold his dog's good name, deserves to be remembered; he was a man who believed in his dog.

Our thots on this occasion also turn to a grave in a St. Louis cemetery where lies buried the then young lawyer, George Graham Vest, of nearby Sedalia, Missouri, whose words before the jury in the old courthouse on the hill above us, have immortalized him and glorified man's best friend so that millions upon millions of dog owners gain from reading these words a new appreciation of their dogs.

Today as we gather to perpetuate the memory of the tribute given to the dog by Senator George Graham Vest before a court jury in this very county seat almost a hundred years ago—in 1870—and to honor the memory of the hound Old Drum, whose killing brot on the four court trials, I think it entirely fitting to carry on with the conclusion that the dog judged as a dog is superior to the human judged as a human in many of the cardinal virtues and surely in conduct and personality.

Some years ago I wrote a book titled Don't Call a Man a Dog; it was based mainly on a lecture of that title which I had been delivering on various occasions. The main conclusion was that when the virtues and merits of the canine are compared to those of the human biped mammal, the dog comes out of the comparison not only as 'man's best friend' but as man's superior friend.

It is customary to refer to the dog and other animals as the 'dumb' creation; but it is man who originated the phrase; we yet have to hear from some of the dumb creation what they think of man. I consider it fortunate for man that the animals are dumb and can not speak in words. I know it is an oft exprest wish that dogs could talk; alas and alack, may that day never arrive! for then we humans will be castigated for what we really are.

Also, is there really any need to add more probable gossip and tongue wagging to that already suffered by us? Why not permit the dog to continue his wagging entirely with his tail? That appendage is one of the most expressive things in the world and enables the dog to talk at both ends.

Seldom do we think of the alfabet of letters as an invention; yet it truly was one and being one, is the most important of all the inventions mankind has come upon since the world began. Our own English-American alfabet has 26 characters and 44 sounds; yet with this low number, our dictionaries contain upward of 700,000 word combinations and with these 44 sounds, noted by codes of letters of the alfabet, all our vast literature has been created, our ideas and ideals have been promulgated, our daily conversation is carried on—and we live as creatures of mind and soul rather than merely of body.

But mark you well, our friend the dog, of whom we expect much, still is back in the primeval ooze of creation insofar as the use of an alfabet is concerned. He of all the species of animal life, makes most use of his voice by way of variations to express his emotions and desires. I have coded the bark and whinings of my own dogs into ten distinct categories.

The dog is taught to obey commands by sounds rather than by words; by tone of voice, by pitch of voice, aided by gesture; thus ear and eye are the chief avenues by which the dog contacts the human, in a strenuous effort to ascertain just what the human wants him to do.

Keep in mind the awful truth that three out of four times you punish your dog, you do so unjustly for he has not been able to understand clearly what you wanted him to do. He can comprehend only thru his dog mind and dog eyes; hence the cardinal commandment in dog pedagogy and training is to look at all situations not as the trainer sees them but as they appear to the dog with his limited capabilities. I verily believe that often it is dumb man and not dumb dog when a dog does not respond to a command.

You can teach a dog to get up by use of the words 'lie down.' Or vice versa. Words in themselves mean nothing to the dog's mental preceptions. My whole point is that the dog without alfabet and coded sounds, has done a splendid job of understanding humans and that the dog is to be praised for valiantly bridging this speech gap between the human and dumb creations.

If the alfabet never had been come upon by some ancient peoples, all of us still would be shrieking and yapping just as the beasts of the jungle do today. This address I am delivering at the very moment would be impossible. The whole world of books and printing would never exist. I could not tell you that this is Warrensburg, Mo., nor could I express any sentiment, idea or thot to you. Yet our dogs are shackled with that same defect; nevertheless they understand us far better than we understand them. Don't call a dog dumb—it's likely your dumbness that does not enable the dog to understand you.

Following on with the title of my discourse—the disadvantages of being a dog. I present a physical matter which too often is not considered as a main factor in elevating the human race to its high position today until it delites to refer to itself as the noblest creation of God and as sons of God. This physical possession is the thumb, the modest thumb, with of course its four companions the fingers.

No animal species approaches the human in the shape and use of the hand, two hands, each with thumb and fingers, which can adjust themselves, work separately or together, and in general, enable the human to do the ten thousand things he does every day with his hands. A few species make more use of their foot appendages than do the others and it is to be noted that these species are a bit more keen, able and self-protecting.

The dog tries earnestly to make use of his paws; yet is sorely limited. Were the human equally limited, it is hardly possible for us to conceive how many things we could not do which now we do unthinkingly as matter of course thru the centuries. The use of all machinery would be impossible; housework, office work, cultivation of fields, acts of transportation, manufacture of goods, the running of printing presses, even our modes of eating, dressing and greeting with a handshake were beyond ability. It can be said that 95% of what we do as humans we would not and could not do, had we paws or hoofs or feet as have animals and had we not the human hand with its pliable thumb and fingers.

The student of the history of the human race must agree that the two things—the alfabet and the human hand have been the two chief possessions which have brot the human species out of the juggle, off the trees and from the caves, and made possible the advancement of the biped mammal man until he is or can be just a little lower than the heavenly creation.

But our friend the dog has not these two advantages. Indeed, let us consider all animals of fields and wilds. Whereas man, mighty man, has devised one instrument of death after another, each one more killing than the previous one—from club to spear to arrow to gun to bomb to atom rays, and whereas the noble sportsman ventures into the fields with high-powered telescopic rifle or even sits in an airplane, rifle in hand, the beasts of the field have no new weapons, no additional means of defense. They still are on the same level as they were ten thousand years ago.

It might not be out of place logically, just as today we are closing National Dog Week thruout America, to have a National Animal Hunt Week when all the animals would be equipped with all the weapons of attack man has and man be the un-armed game for the week. That would be sporting indeed. I have only sympathy and admiration for the hunted animal of the field and forest. The great odds against him eliminate any element of the true meaning of the term sporting chance.

Judge a man not so much by his costly home, his large bank account or his fine clothes as by the way he treats his dog. Who kicks a dog, really kicks his own soul into hell.

My Dog

AUTHOR'S NOTE—In the 30's decade we were member of a committee to choose the ten best dog poems of the year. Out of more than 1,100 submitted, this was chosen as one of the ten best and thru the author's persistence, it won first prize. He has never regretted his persistence.

Through glad days and sad days
We two have clung together;
O'er rough roads and tough roads
In every kind of weather.
Our square meals and spare meals
Have both been shared together;
On warm nights and storm nights
We've slept amongst the heather.
A fair friend, a rare friend
Who never asks me whether
It's byways or highways
Just so we are together.

—WM. H. RUMSEY (written in 1934 by this Penna. poet at the age of 80).

TRIBUTE TO DOG—1200 A.D.

(From the book Medieval Lore by Robert Steele)

Nothing is more busy and wittier than a hound, for he hath more wit than other beasts.

And hounds know their own names, and love their masters, and defend the houses of their masters, and put themselves wilfully in peril of death for their masters, and run to take prey for their masters, and forsake not the dead bodies of their masters.

We have known that hounds fought for their lords against thieves, and were sore wounded, and that they kept away beasts and fowls from their masters' bodies dead. And that a hound compelled the slayer of his master with barking and biting to acknowledge his trespass and guilt.

The Power of the Dog

AUTHOR'S NOTE—It is a pleasure to include this famed poem on a dog's love in this anthology and scrapbook of ultra-selected items, that is, only the best of the best.

RUDYARD KIPLING has an advantage against us for we are a burning devotee of almost all he wrote; yet this English poet and story-teller here has exprest in one of his traditional exotic styles, what every dog owner feels as old age whitens the muzzle, slows the step and stiffens the hindquarters of a member of the family, the dog.

When His Majesty the Dog came into the household, he was a gay and bouncing pup, so full of life that even the young children scarce could keep up the play. Now, they are grown up, yes—but still in the very prime of young manhood and womanhood, starting a new phase of human life.

The dog's life has paralleled theirs only in time for now he is a tired old man, his race almost run, his allotted span soon to have its end, on the basis of the tragic, nature-decreed ratio of seven to one—now at ten, he's as old as his former playmates just in their mid-teens will be at seventy.

Pity the old dog; give him an extra pat as he stretches out for nite's sleep; tomorrow you may pat him on the head as has been your wont thru the years, but no adoring eyes open, no tail wags in response.

There is sorrow enough in the natural way
From men and women to fill our day;
But when we are certain of sorrow in store,
Why do we always arrange for more?
Brothers and sisters, I bid you beware
OF GIVING YOUR HEART TO A DOG TO TEAR!

We've sorrow enough in the natural way,
When it comes to burying Christian clay.
Our loves are not given, but only lent,
At compound interest at cent per cent.
Though it is not always the case, I believe,
That the longer we've kept 'em, the more do we grieve:
For, when debts are payable, right or wrong,
A short time loan is as bad as a long—
So why in Heaven (before we are there)
SHOULD WE GIVE OUR HEARTS TO A DOG TO TEAR?

Buy a pup and your money will buy
Love unflinching that cannot lie—
Perfect passion and worship fed
By a kick in the ribs or a pat on the head.
Nevertheless, it is hardly fair
TO RISK YOUR HEART FOR A DOG TO TEAR.

When the fourteen years that Nature permits
Are closing in asthma, or tumor, or fits,
And the vet's unspoken prescription runs
To lethal chambers or loaded guns,
Then you will find—it's your own affair,
BUT . . . YOU'VE GIVEN YOUR HEART TO A DOG TO TEAR.

When the body that lived at your single will,
When the whimper of welcome is stilled (how still!);
When the spirit that answered your every mood
Is gone—wherever it goes—for good,
You will discover how much you care
AND WILL GIVE YOUR HEART TO A DOG TO TEAR.

Dogs as Companions

They are much superior to human beings as companions. They do not quarrel or argue with you. They never talk about themselves but listen to you while you talk about yourself, and keep up an appearance of being interested in the conversation. They never make stupid remarks and they never ask a young author with fourteen tragedies, sixteen comedies, several farces, and a couple of burlesques in his desk, why he doesn't write a play.

They never say unkind things. They never tell us our faults, "merely for our own good." They do not at inconvenient moments mildly remind us of our past follies and mistakes.

They never inform us, like our inamoratas sometimes do, that we are not nearly so nice as we used to be. We are always the same to them.

He is very imprudent, a dog is. He never makes it his business to inquire whether you are in the right or in the wrong, never bothers as to whether you are going up or down upon life's ladder, never asks whether you are rich or poor, silly or wise, sinner or saint. You are his pal. That is enough for him, and come luck or misfortune, good repute or bad, honor or shame, he is going to stick to you, to comfort you, guard you, give his life for you, if need be—foolish, brainless, soulless dog!—*Jerome K. Jerome* in Idle Thoughts Of An Idle Fellow.

Epitaph to a Dog

(On a monument in the garden of Newstead Abbey, England)

NEAR THIS SPOT
ARE DEPOSITED THE REMAINS
OF ONE
WHO POSSESSED BEAUTY
WITHOUT VANITY,
STRENGTH WITHOUT INSOLENCE,
COURAGE WITHOUT FEROCITY,
AND ALL THE VIRTUES OF MAN
WITHOUT HIS VICES.

THIS PRAISE, WHICH WOULD BE UNMEANING
FLATTERY
IF INSCRIBED OVER HUMAN ASHES,
IS BUT A JUST TRIBUTE TO THE MEMORY OF
"BOATSWAIN," A DOG
WHO WAS BORN AT NEWFOUNDLAND
MAY, 1803
AND DIED AT NEWSTEAD ABBEY
NOV. 18, 1808

When some proud son of man returns to earth,
Unknown to glory, but upheld by birth,
The sculptor's art exhausts the pomp of woe,
And storied urns record who rests below;
When all is done, upon the tomb is seen,
Not what he was, but what he should have been.
But the poor dog, in life the firmest friend,
The first to welcome, foremost to defend,
Whose honest heart is still his master's own,
Who labors, fights, lives breathes for him alone,
Unhonored falls, unnoticed all his worth,
Denied in heaven the soul he held on earth—
While man, vain insect! hopes to be forgiven,
And claims himself a sole exclusive heaven.
Oh man! thou feeble tenant of an hour,
Debased by slavery, or corrupt by power—
Who knows thee well must quit thee with disgust,
Degraded mass of animated dust!
Thy love is lust, thy friendship all a cheat,
Thy smiles hyprocrisy, thy words deceit!
By nature vile, ennobled but by name,
Each kindred brute might bid thee blush for shame.

"BRENDON BLONDE VENUS".
Bred by Mrs. Adlam and owned by Captain Goldsmith, "Blonde Venus" in 1934 was considered one of the best Coloured Bull Terrier bitches exhibited.

"BRENDON DRAGON".
Mrs. G. M. Adlam's remarkable brindle dog won the Lady Winifred Challenge Cup for the best Coloured Bull Terrier at Cruft's in 1934.

PUPPY DAYS.

Two Bull Terrier puppies, owned by Mr. Dugald McGregor—one showing a good type of head—are playing together and taking it very seriously.

Ye, who perchance behold this simple urn,
Pass on—it honors none you wish to mourn.
To mark a friend's remains these stones arise;
I never knew but one—and there he lies.

—LORD BYRON

Constancy

You don't need riches,
  You don't need looks,
You needn't have read
  A line in books,
You don't need purple,
  You don't need fame—
Your dog will love you
  Just the same!
You may lack money,
  An ugly wight
Without the sense to
  Come in at night,
You may be ragged,
  And have no name—
Your dog will love you
  Just the same!

—FRED B. MANN

CH. DELPHINIUM WILD.

Little Dog Angel

High up in the courts of heaven today
The little dog angel waits.
With the other angels he will not play
But he sits alone at the gates.
For I know that my master will come, says he,
And when he comes he will call for me.
And his master, far in the world below,
As he sits in his easy chair,
Forgets himself and whistles low
For the dog—that is not there.
And the little dog angel cocks his ears
And dreams that his master's voice he hears.
And I know, some day, when his master waits
Outside in the dark and cold
For the hand of death to open the gates
That lead to those courts of gold,
The little dog angel's eager bark
Will comfort his soul while he's still in the dark.

—NORAH M. HOLLAND

Pals

Hurrah!
Here they come!
Heralded loud by fife and drum,
The Boy and his Pal in proud parade!
The Boy is nonchalant, unafraid,
Heir of the Ages! Fronting life,
Ready to tilt with toil and strife.
And the Pal? He keeps his chum in sight,
Barking to left and barking to right,
And the two, as they march, proclaim to all,
"We are Boy and Dog, and Pal and Pal!"
Hurrah!
Watch them jog!
Wonderful creatures! Boy and Dog!

—SUSIE H. BEST

The Little Black Dog

I wonder if Christ had a little black dog,
All curly and woolly like mine,
With two long silk ears and a nose round and wet,
And two eyes brown and tender that shine.
I'm sure if He had, that little black dog
Knew right from the first He was God,
That he needed no proof that Christ was divine,
But just worshipped the ground He trod.
I'm afraid that He hadn't, because I have read
How He prayed in the Garden alone,
When all of His friends and disciples had fled,
Even Peter, that one called a stone.
And oh, I am sure that little black dog
With a true heart so tender and warm
Would never have left Him to suffer alone,
But creep right under His arm;
Would have licked those dear fingers in agony clasped,
And counting all favors but loss,
When they led Him away, would have trotted behind
And followed Him quite to the cross.

—ELIZABETH GARDNER REYNOLDS

(With special permission of Good Housekeeping)

Proverbs and Bits of Wisdom about Dogs

The more I see of men, the better I like my dog.—FREDERICK THE GREAT *(of his Italian greyhound).*

"God created man; then seeing how weak he was, gave him the dog."—TOUSSENEL.

For my part, I do wish thou wert a dog, that I might love thee.
—SHAKESPEARE.

Whenever a man is unhappy, God sends him a dog.
—LAMARTINE.

Dog is the only animal that loves you more than he loves himself.—OLD SAYING.

EPITAPH FOR A SMALL DOG

Here rests a little dog
Whose feet ran never faster
Than when they took the path
Leading to his master.
—LEBARON COOKE.

EPITAPH ON A FAVORITE DOG

Thou who passest on the path; if haply thou dost mark this monument, laugh not I pray thee, though it is a dog's grave; tears fell for me and the dust was heaped above me by a master's hands who likewise engraved these words on my tomb.—*From Greek literature (about 350 B. C.)*

EPITAPH ON A DOG'S TOMBSTONE NEAR CHEVY CHASE, M.D., (1940)

"Dear Master:

I've explained to St. Peter, I'd rather stay here, outside of the pearly gates. I won't be a nuisance, I won't even bark. I'll be very patient and wait. I'll lie here and chew a celestial bone, no matter how long you may be. I miss you so much. If I went in alone, it wouldn't be heaven for me."

WHEN THE DOG'S SOUL COMES THRU HIS EYES

If a man does not soon pass beyond the thought "By what shall this dog profit me?" into the large state of simple gladness to be with dog, he shall never know the very essence of that companionship which depends not on the points of dog, but on some strange and subtle mingling of mute spirits. For it is by muteness that a dog becomes for one so utterly beyond value. With him one is at peace where words play no torturing tricks. When he just sits loving and knows that he is being loved, those are the moments that I think are precious to a dog: when, with his adoring soul coming through his eyes, he feels that you are really thinking of him.—JOHN GALSWORTHY in Memories.

HOW BENVENUTO CELLINI'S DOG IDENTIFIED A ROBBER

Happening just about this time to pass by the square of Navona with my fine shock-dog, as soon as I came to the door of the city marshal, the dog barked very loudly and flew at a young man, who had been arrested by one Donnino, a goldsmith of Parma, formerly a pupil of Caradosso, upon suspicion of having committed a robbery. My dog made such efforts to tear this young fellow to pieces that he roused the city-guards.

The prisoner asserted his innocence boldly, and Donnino did not say so much as he ought to have done, especially as I was present. There happened likewise to be by one of the chief officers of the city-guard, who was a Genoese, and well acquainted with the prisoner's father; insomuch that on account of the violence offered by the dog, and for other reasons, they were for dismissing the youth, as if he had been innocent.

As soon as I came up, the dog, which dreaded neither swords nor sticks, again flew at the young man. The guards told me that if I did not keep off my dog they would kill it. I called off the dog with some difficulty, and as the young man was retiring, certain little paper bundles fell from under the cape of his cloak, which Donnino immediately discovered to belong to him.

Amongst them I perceived a little ring which I knew to be my property: whereupon I said: 'This is the villain that broke open my shop, and my dog knows him again.' I therefore let the dog loose, and he once more seized the thief, who then implored mercy, and told me he would restore me whatever he had of mine. On this I again called off my dog, and the fellow returned me all the gold, silver, and rings that he had robbed me of, and gave me five-and-twenty crowns over, imploring my forgiveness.—BENVENUTO CELLINI.

(from *Memoirs*, ending in 1562.)

DOGS IN HOTELS

We have received numerous copies of the following, which was written to a hotel manager asking whether or not he would accept a guest with a dog. Here is the letter, and it certainly is worth publishing many times:

"*I've been in business for 30 yrs. Never have I called on police to eject a disorderly dog. Never has a dog set fire to a bed with a cigarette. I have never found a hotel towel or blanket in a dog's suitcase—nor a whiskey ring on a dog's dresser. Sure, the dog is welcome.*"

How Baron Munchausen's Dog Tray Had His Honor Upheld

In a voyage which I made to the East Indies with Captain Hamilton, I took a favourite pointer with me; he was, to use a common phrase, worth his weight in gold, for he never deceived me. One day when we were, by the best observations that we could make, at least 300 leagues from land, my dog pointed. I watched him for nearly an hour with astonishment, and mentioned the circumstance to the Captain, and to every officer on board, asserting that we must be near land, for my dog smelt game. This occasioned a general laugh; but that did not alter in the least the good opinion I had of my dog.

After much conversation pro and con, I boldly told the Captain I placed more confidence in Tray's nose than I did in the eyes of every seaman on board, and therefore boldly proposed laying the sum I had agreed to pay for my passage (viz., 100 guineas) that we should find game within half an hour.

The Captain (a good hearty fellow) laughed again, and desired Mr. Crawford, the surgeon, who was prepared, to feel my pulse; he did so, and reported me in perfect health. The following dialogue between them took place; I overheard it, though spoken low and at some distance:

CAPTAIN. His brain is turned; I cannot with honour accept his wager.

SURGEON. I am of a different opinion; he is quite sane, and depends more upon the scent of his dog than he will upon the judgment of all the officers on board; he will certainly lose, and he richly merits it.

CAPTAIN. Such a wager cannot be fair on my side; however, I'll take him up, if I return his money afterwards.

During the above conversation, Tray continued in the same situation, and confirmed me still more in my former opinion. I proposed the wager a second time; it was then accepted.

Done! and done! were scarcely said on both sides when some sailors who were fishing in the long-boat, which was made fast to the stern of the ship, harpooned an exceedingly large shark, which they brought on board and began to cut up for the purpose of barrelling the oil, when, behold, they found no less than six brace of live partridges in the creature's stomach.

They had been so long in that situation that one of the hens was sitting upon four eggs, and a fifth was hatching when the shark was opened! This young bird we brought up, by placing it with a litter of kittens that came into the world a few minutes before. The old cat was as fond of it as of any of her own four-legged progeny, and made herself very unhappy when it flew out of her reach until it returned again.

As to the other partridges, there were four hens amongst them; one or more were, during the voyage, constantly sitting, and consequently we had plenty of game at the Captain's table; and in gratitude to poor Tray (for being a means of winning 100 guineas) I ordered him the bones daily, and sometimes a whole bird.

—RUDOLF ERICH RASPE

(From *Original Travels and Surprising Adventures of Baron Munchausen*, 1785, trans, anon. 1889.)

Rip Van Winkle's Dog Wolf

Rip's sole domestic adherent was his dog Wolf, who was as much henpecked as his master; for Dame Van Winkle regarded them as companions in idleness, and even looked upon Wolf with an evil eye as the cause of his master's going so often astray. True it is, in all points of spirit befitting an honourable dog, he was as courageous an animal as ever scoured the woods—but what courage can withstand the ever-during and all-besetting terrors of a woman's tongue?

The moment Wolf entered the house, his crest fell, his tail drooped to the ground, or curled between his legs, he sneaked about with a gallows air, casting many a sidelong glance at Dame Van Winkle, and at the least flourish of a broomstick or ladle, he would fly to the door with yelping precipitation. . . .

Poor Rip was at last reduced almost to despair, and his only alternative to escape from the labour of the farm and clamour of his wife, was to take gun in hand, and stroll away into the woods. Here he would sometimes seat himself at the foot of a tree, and share the contents of his wallet with Wolf, with whom he sympathized as a fellow-sufferer in persecution. 'Poor Wolf,' he would say, 'thy mistress leads thee a dog's life of it; but never mind, my lad, whilst I live thou shalt never want a friend to stand by thee!' Wolf would wag his tail, look wistfully in his master's face, and if dogs can feel pity, I verily believe he reciprocated the sentiment with all his heart.—WASHINGTON IRVING (from *Rip Van Winkle*, in *The Sketch Book*), 1820.

A BOY AND A DOG

I want my boy to have a dog
Or maybe two or three
He'll learn from them much easier
Than he would learn from me.
A dog will show him how to love
And bear no grudge or hate
I'm not so good at that myself
But dogs will do it straight.
I want my boy to have a dog
To be his pal and friend
So he may learn that friendship
Is faithful to the end.
There never yet has been a dog
Who learned to doublecross
Nor catered to you when you won
Then dropped you when you lost.

—Marty Hale, *The Old Spinner*

THROUGH SUNLIT FIELDS

(Poetical Reverie of a "Bird Dog" Man)

Through sunlit fields I sometimes stride
My stalwart pointers by my side.
The joy of life sings through each vein,
Who would not thrill to its refrain
While carefree roaming meadows wide,
The fall is o'er and now betide
On city sidewalks I must stride,
No more my pointers dash amain
Through sunlit fields.
But when in winters even'tide
I loll and doze by fire beside,
Imagination has free rein
And then I see myself again,
On mem'ries magic carpet ride
Through sunlit fields.

—EDWARD DANA KNIGHT

FOR A LITTLE BOY

I want to give a little boy—such an important little boy—something that will show him FAITH, alive and glowing.

I want to give a little boy something that will teach the spirit of him the glorious virtue of unselfish COURAGE.

I want to give a little boy something that will impress upon his clean heart and spirit every day, every night, every hour of the day and night the mighty power and exquisite beauty of LOVE.

I want to teach a little boy the importance of, and the reason for, DISCIPLINE.

And so—I am going to give a little boy a little dog, and what a gay and happy time a little boy and a little dog and a devoted dad will have! What a lovely and fascinating and interesting school we will attend—we three together!—R. A. Grady.

"CHILDREN-DOG RECIPE"

Take one large grassy field,
One half-dozen children,
Two or three small dogs,
A pinch of brook
And some pebbles—

Mix the children and dogs well together, then put them in the field, stirring constantly. Pour the brook over the pebbles. Sprinkle the field with flowers. Spread over all a deep blue sky, and bake in the hot sun. When brown, remove and set away in a bathtub to cool.—*Author unfortunately unknown.*

WHEN CAESAR MARCHED BEHIND HIS KING

When were kings compelled to march behind a dog?

When King Edward VII of England died in 1910, it was learned he had given stern instructions that his pet foxterrier named Caesar march directly behind the artillery caisson carrying his body. Edward even threatened to haunt any one who disobeyed this order.

And so it happened—Caesar marched behind his master's body; and kings, potentates, prime ministers and Emperor Kaiser Wilhelm of Germany marched behind the little terrier.

Caesar himself lived to the ripe age of 14 years and was buried in a bronze casket at Fort Rudd, England.

A POMPEII HERO

About thirty years ago (1925 AD) certain men were excavating in Pompeii, that Italian City which, in the first century, was suddenly destroyed by an eruption of the volcano "Vesuvius."

Outside a dwelling they discovered the body of a small lad as if he had fallen asleep. The little chap had been overtaken by the clouds of poison gas and torrents of red-hot ashes from the mountain.

Beside the boy was a big dog with its teeth caught in its master's cloak. It looked as though the dog had made a great effort to save the boy.

Around the dog's neck was a big silver collar. The metal was all tarnished, but when cleaned it was seen to have this inscription in Latin: "This dog has thrice saved the life of his little master. Once from fire, once from water, and once from thieves."

Even at this last hour, when destruction poured down from the sky, it was plain that the faithful animal had tried to save his little master a fourth time.—From *Tail-Wagger Magazine* (London).

DOGS ON THE ROMAN FARM

Nor let the care of dogs be last in your thoughts; feed swift Spartan whelps and fierce Molossians alike on fattening whey. Never, with them on guard, need you fear in your stalls a midnight thief, nor onslaught of wolves, nor restless Spaniards behind your back.—Virgil—(From the *Georgies* III, trans. H. R. Fairclough), 30 B.C.

WHAT BREED WAS IT?

There is a certain strong breed of hunting-dogs, small, but worthy of a sublime song, which the wild tribes of painted Britons maintain, and they call them gaze-hounds. Their size, indeed, is about that of the worthless pampered domestic tabledogs, crooked, slight, shaggy, dull-eyed, but furnished with numerous envenomed teeth, and their feet armed with formidable nails.

The gaze-hound excels above all in his nose; he is first-rate for tracing, since he is very sagacious in finding the track of animals over the ground, and moreover, expert in indicating the very odour that floats in the air. —Oppian of Apamea (from *Cynegetica,* C. 215 A.D.).

'AWAY FROM CIVILIZATION, WHAT DOES ONE NEED MOST?'

That was the title of an essay contest which the Chicago Daily News ran about the year 1940. The prize letter was written by one who said he would take a dog with him.

Because of its excellence in both sentiment and literary style, we reprint it here from Dog World.

• • •

If I had to spend a long time away from civilization and could take only one thing with me I would certainly take something alive, preferably a dog.

The reasons for this are because of his unwavering loyalty, his sense of responsibility as regards his master's person and belongings, his extremely acute sense of approaching danger and the absolute adoration that even a mongrel is capable of giving his owner.

More than anything alive, the dog seems to fill the need of a close affectionate honest friend. Therefore I would take a dog.

There is nothing in his mechanism to go static. There is nothing forced or mechanic about his feeling for you. There is no danger which he will not share willingly. He will never be disgustingly drunk. Neither will insist upon talking when you desire quiet. And no matter how soundly he may seem to be sleeping—if you need him he is right there every time.

I would take a dog because if, away from civilization, death should chance to be my lot, I could pass on happier in the knowledge that while life remained in his faithful body my dog would still be my champion, my defender. I am sure I would sleep the sweeter knowing that he was lying above me whispering "Peace, old pal, on the long, long trek."

"ON THE SLY"

One thing my wife and I've said over
And over—we will not feed Rover
At table, even though he begs
And nuzzles up against our legs
And toward us is forever turning
Those looks of hunger, hurt, and yearning . .
We have agreed and that is why
We only do it on the sly.

—RICHARD ARMOUR.

LOYALTY

(Reprinted from Dog World, 1924)

A man may lose his house and lot,
His friends may pass him by,
He may not have a thin dime left
To rent a slab of pie;

But if he owns the homeliest
And saddest dog in town,
He has one pal whose honest love
Will never turn him down.

A man may kick his mangy pup
And cuss him day and night,
Still will the faithful cur be true
And greet him with delight.

Life long he sits upon the porch
And wags his happy tail,
To greet his lord when he shall come
From Congress or from jail.

LIKE CHILD, LIKE PUPPY

Owning a dog is a serious responsibility. To enjoy the position of dog's master incurs obligation. The dog surrenders many of his natural rights and habits in return for the servitude he gives the human.

The puppy is the perfect example of trusting loyalty. To him the world's a stranger to be greeted. Not only each day but each moment of each hour of the day, he discovers something new in our world of humans, in which he must live.

Life is an endless chain experience of play, discovery and thrills. Not a care worries his carefree soul. What scene on this earth holds more pure happiness than that of a litter of playing puppies—brothers and sisters in a family world that has not yet known separation!

Consequently, a puppy, particularly if it is brot into a new home, should receive every consideration in the way of feeding, care, housing and training. At three months of age, it compares with the infant just out of the cradle; and to a great extent the same care which the child receives, should be given to the puppy.—

GREAT FRIEND MAKER

Dale Carnegie, whose book How to Make Friends and Influence People has been a best seller, wrote: "Why read my book to find out how to win friends?" Why not study the technique of the greatest winner of friends the world has ever known? You may meet him coming down the street. When you get within ten feet of him he will begin to wag his tail. If you stop and pat him he will almost jump out of his skin to show how much he likes you.

And you know that behind this show of affection on his part, there are no ulterior motives; he has nothing to sell and doesn't want to marry you.

"Did you ever stop to think that a dog is the only animal that does not have to work for a living? A hen has to lay eggs; a cow has to give milk; and a canary has to sing. But a dog makes his living by giving you nothing but love."

Sweet Lavender.

STEPHENS ON HIS DOG

A friend called attention to the inscription Alexander H. Stephens, Vice-President of the Confederacy, placed on a tombstone in a little plot where his dogs were buried. It reads:

"Here rest the remains of what in life
Was a satire upon the human race,
But an ornament to his own—a faithful dog."

WALKING WITH A DOG HAS EXTRA PLEASURE

You will generally fare better to take your dog than invite your neighbor.

Your dog is a true pedestrian, and your neighbor is very likely a small politician. The dog enters thoroughly into the spirit of the enterprise; he is not indifferent or preoccupied; he is constantly sniffing adventure, laps at every spring, looks upon every field and wood as a new world to be explored, is ever on some fresh trail, knows something important will happen a little farther on, gazes with the true wonder-seeing eyes, whatever the spot or whatever the road, finds it good to be there—in short, is just that happy, delicious, excursive vagabond that touches one at so many points, and whose human prototype in a companion robs miles and leagues of half their power to fatigue.—JOHN BURROUGHS.

IF YOU CAN'T FIND THE PERFECT MAN, OWN A DOG

"And there is more than one woman—even a beautiful woman—who has never found the man to love the pilgrim soul in her; and, after passionate protestations and broken vows, old, disillusioned, sad, and deserted, she has regained faith in love and fidelity thru the devotion of a dog.

"He does not change when beauty flees, nor when poverty comes, nor when health goes. He gives his heart, his true and single heart to his mistress forever.

"She may be old and gray, with furrowed face, but he sees the pilgrim soul in her."—Mrs. T. P. O'Connor in her book Dog Stars.

WHEN DACHS' EYES ARE DIM WITH LOVE

The dachshund's trusting eyes are dim
With love for you—and tender;
The dachshund is so long and slim
And slithery and slender
That when you pat his head on Sunday
His little tail won't wag till Monday
Hoot Mon! And also Teckelheil.

—BERTHA BRIGHT RAINGER

MY OLD HOUND PACK

When my hunting here is over
From the tall harps' golden sounds
I will steal away to hearken
To the voices of the hounds.
When they start a phantom red fox
On a phantom heavenly hill,
And with me, a phantom huntsman,
Getting all the old-time thrill.
For a man who's bred to hunting
Must forever be that way;
And he'll never know it's heaven
Till he listens, and can say:
"There's a short low tenor,
And a yipping ki-yi;
There's a bell-mouth ringing
That a fox has got to die.
There's a ding-dong chop-mouth,
Always in the noise;
There's a bass with no bottom,
And a rolling gong voice.
There's a bugle with a break,
And a bugle with a scream,
And a high wailing tenor
Like a trumpet in a dream!"
—ARCHIBALD RUTLEDGE.

A GERMAN COMEDIAN'S SOLILOQUY ON THE DOG

"Vot's der matter mit a dog's life anyhow? Look at my dog Towser layin' by der fire. Is his life bad? He chust et some bones und his belly is full. Me—I got indispeption and can't eat nuddings. Und I gotta hurry back to work. Towser eats und hurries back to sleep.

"I gotta buy school books und pants for my four children. He's got maybe 40 children. Does he have to buy them school books und pants? No, he don't.

"But even worse when he dies, he's a dead dog und that's all mit him. Me—after I get dead, I gotta go to hell, yet besides!"

A PRAYER FOR ANIMALS

Hear our humble prayer O God for our friends the animals who are suffering—for all that are overworked, underfed and cruelly treated.

For any that are hunted, lost or deserted, frightened or hungry.

For all that are in pain or dying.

For all that must be put to sleep—we entreat for them Thy mercy and pity.

For all those who deal with them we ask a heart of compassion, gentle hands and kindly words.

Make us ourselves true friends of animals and may we share the blessings of the merciful for the sake of Thy Son—the tender hearted Healer—Jesus Christ our Lord. Amen!

(Copied from the original in the Children's Corner in Berwick Church, Sussex, England.)

THE DOG BELIEVED IN SIGNS

Ah! you should keep dogs—fine animals—sagacious creatures—dog of my own once—pointer—surprising instinct—out shooting one day—entering enclosure—whistled—dog stopped—whistled again—Ponto—no go; stock still—called him—Ponto, Ponto—wouldn't move—dog transfixed—staring at a board—looked up; saw an inscription—"Gamekeeper has orders to shoot all dogs found in this enclosure"—wouldn't pass it—wonderful dog—valuable dog that—very.—Mr. Fingle, in Charles Dickens' Pickwick Papers.

CUVIER ON DOGS

"The domestic dog," said Cuvier, the great natural scientist, "is the most complete, the most singular, and the most useful conquest that man has gained in the animal world.

"The whole species has become our property; each individual belongs entirely to his master, acquires his disposition, knows and defends his property, and remains attached to until death; and all this, not through constraint or necessity, but purely by the influences of gratitude and real attachment.

"The swiftness, the strength, the sharp scent of the dog, have rendered him a powerful ally to man against the lower tribes, and were, perhaps, necessary for the establishment of the dominion of mankind over the whole animal creation.

"The dog is the only animal which has followed man over the whole earth."

MOTTO FOR A DOG HOUSE

I love this little house because
It offers, after dark,
A pause for rest, a rest for paws,
A place to moor my bark.
—*Arthur Guiterman.*

REST IN PEACE

Father, in Thy starry tent,
I kneel, a humble suppliant,
A dog has died today on earth—
Of little worth
Yet very dear.
Gather him in Thy arms,
If only
For awhile,
I fear
He will be lonely,
Shield him with Thy smile.
—*Wilfred J. Funk.*

THE LOVER OF DOGS

He made and loveth all.
Both man and bird and beast!
He prayeth best who loveth best
All things both great and small!
For the dear God who loveth us,
He made and loveth all.
—S. T. COLERIDGE.

THE DEAD DOG THAT CAME BACK

We have published many stories of dogs that returned far distances from their homes to their old homes. Here's a new twist to an old story.

An AP dispatch of Apr 28, '54, from Houston, Texas, tells of a four-year-old cocker that had been struck by an automobile on Apr 11. The owner decided the injured dog should be put to sleep and the veterinarian did so on April 14. The veterinarian buried the dog.

Thirteen days later, Apr. 27, 'Stray,' for that was the dog's name, scratched at the door of his owner's home, 30 miles from the place where he had been buried. The owner almost fainted when she saw the dog. She called the veterinarian. 'I trembled all over,' the vet'n said. 'It was Stray, allright; only instead of his usual red hair, he was covered from head to tail with dirt, a dirty bandage dangling from the hind leg.'

Certainly, this cocker deserved the steak with the big bone, which the vet'n ordered prepared for him by the best chef in Houston. —

LUCKIEST DOG OF THE YEAR

Down in Rossville, Ga. on Oct. 7, there was just about to happen the tragedy of the chained dog—the faithful watchdog who gives warning that the house is on fire. The occupants run out to safety but the dog remains tied in the burning house.

A 5-yr.-old hound was chained under a burning house in Rossville; he howled helplessly for rescue, but the flames kept the would-be rescuers back.

A passerby from Georgia stopped off to see the fire, saw the dog's plight, seized a shotgun and fired at the dog's head in order to kill him and put him out of the suffering.

Here is the finale—"The pellets only clipped the dog's collar; and Butch the hound dashed off to a nearby creek to cool himself in the waters."—

SCOTCH DOG

A Scotsman had a *dog*, and each morning he gave him a penny to buy a bun. The dog deposited his penny each time in his kennel till he had five. Then off he went to the baker's shop and bought six buns for a nickel.

LOYALTY

"You can't buy loyalty," they say;
I bought it though this very day.
You can't buy friendship, firm and true.
I bought sincerest friendship, too,
And truth and kindliness I got
And happiness, oh, such a lot,
So many joyous hours-to-be
Were sold with this commodity.

"I bought a life of simple faith
And love that will be mine till death;
And two brown eyes that I could see
Would not be long in knowing me.
I bought protection, I've a guard
Right now and ever afterward.
Buy human friendship? Maybe not—
You see, it was a dog I bought."

—Anne Campbell

NATIONAL DOG WEEK

Few moments in the canine world have been so much publicised and have done so much constructive effort in behalf of better dog care than has national Dog Week. The Week is observed in America during all of the last full week of each September. It is sponsored by the National Dog Week Association.

The seven objectives of the Week are given here. They well can be considered a complete agenda for dog owners and dog lovers in all countries.

1. A good home for every dog.
2. Elimination of stray dogs from the streets.
3. Better informed dog owners.
4. Consideration for dogs and all animals.
5. Emphasis of the dog's use as companion and protector.
6. Fair laws for dogs and dog-owners.
7. Respect for the rights of non-dog-owners.

"MY PUP"

He's a rogue and a rascal,
A pest and a pain
And he wrecks my nylon hose.
He tracks up floors,
And nips at my heels
But I love him, goodness knows!
He annoys my friends,
When they come to call
With his shrill and noisy yap
And before they're settled in a chair
He lunges for a lap.
He simply ignores my mad protest,
And I am at a loss
It's plain for all my guests to see
Exactly who's the boss.
But when he comes at the end of day
And strikes a repentant pose,
I gather him up in my arms to rest
For I love him, goodness knows!

—HELENA DARBY

AN XMAS PUP

A Poodle, A Yorkie
A chubby young Pug
A smart Pekingese
With his quaint little mug,
A Manchester toy
A Papillon rare,
A beloved terrier
That's seen everywhere—
A Maltese, Affenpinscher
Whate'er it may be,
Take your choice,
But remember—
Put a pup 'neath your tree.

—PERLA O. RICHIARDS

PAUL REVERE'S DOG

Now comes word that another individual has been slighted on history's pages. It is a matter of fact that two men made the historic ride on the 18th of April in '75 ("of which hardly a man is now alive"), the other being a Mr. Dawes, ancestor of Vice President Chas Dawes. Paul Revere, jeweler received all the glory.

Esther Forbes in her book Paul Revere and the World He Lived In, reveals the astonishing fact that it was the cleverness and dependability of Paul's dog, coupled with training that would be a credit to an obedience test winner, that made the "midnight ride" of song and story possible.

She even states in so many words that the Revere dog was in a sense, the "hero" of that world-famous "adventure."

GOING TO THE DOGS

My grandpa notes the world's worn cogs,
And says we're going to the dogs;
His grandad in his house of logs,
Swore things were going to the dogs;
His dad, among the Flemish bogs,
Vowed things were going to the dogs;
The caveman in his queer skin togs,
Said things were going to the dogs;
But this is what I wish to state—
The dogs have had an awful wait.

—Anonymous.

MONGREL PUP FROM THE DOG SHOP

"The months crept by, as seasons will, the pup
Grew lank, unlovely as a clump of weeds;
And as he grew, our wonder grew in kind,
That one lone dog could boast so many breeds.
He had an airedale's face, but that was all;
The bagging ears were those of any hound;
His silken coat was eloquent of collie;
And from his tail we knew where he'd been found."

—MAURICE J. RONAYNE

A PROBLEM

What dog to buy?
Which breed to try?
I ponder and ponder—
I worry and sigh!
Long hair? Short hair?
Eyes deep brown, or yellow?
A hunter or collie—
Or just a good fellow?
Do I want a companion,
A guardian—a ratter?
A lap dog to cuddle?
Oh, what does it matter!
Big breed, small breed—
Black, white or brown.
I want a dog
For my very own!
—NAN SWIGERT.

CHRISTMAS PUPPIES

Every single puppy here
Is saying: "Choose me!"
Wagging tail, wiggling ears,—
"Don't refuse me!
"I'm your dog, wide awake!
Won't we have fun?"
Well, we have got to take
Every single one!
—NANCY BYRD TURNER

IN RETROSPECT

Our house is empty, silent now—
I never knew just how
A little dog could fill a place,
Scampering through at breakneck pace,
Scattering rugs—an upset chair—
Confusion reigned most everywhere.
But what I'd give if it could be
That he again would meet and jump on me.
Capt. Ellis Reed-Hill (USCG)
in National Humane Review.

MRS. MONTAGUE STURRIDGE AND HER BULL TERRIER.

Once upon a time the Bull Terrier was a breed debarred from society because it was associated with the gamester, pugilist and dog-fighter; but to-day the Bull Terrier is a member in leading households.

CAPTAIN HOOK, THE SON OF *Ch.* ROMANY RATHER LIGHTLY AND *Ch.* RICKMAY ANBADAAD, AT 2 MONTHS.

Napoleon in Exile Recalls An Incident of the Retreat from Moscow

Suddenly I saw a dog coming out from under the clothes of a corpse. He rushed forward toward us and then returned to his retreat, uttering mournful cries. He licked the face of his master and darted toward us again; it seemed as if he was seeking aid and vengeance at the same time.

Whether it was my state of mind, or the place, the time, the weather, the act itself, or I know not what, never has anything, on all my fields of battle, made such an impression upon me. I stopped involuntarily to contemplate the spectacle; that man, I said to myself, perhaps has friends, perhaps he has them in the camp, in his company, and yet he lies here abandoned by all except his dog.

What is man! and what the mystery of his impressions! I had ordered battles without emotion, battles which were to decide the fate of the army; I had seen, dry-eyed, movements executed which brought about the loss of a great number of our soldiers; here I was moved to tears. What is certain is that at the moment I must have been more favorably disposed toward a suppliant enemy. I better understood Achilles surrendering Hector's body to Priam's tears.

SCOTLAND'S BURNS ON DOGS

Man is the god of the dog; he knows no other; he can understand no other. And see how he worships him! with what reverence he crouches at his feet, with what love he fawns upon him! with what dependence he looks up to him! with what cheerful alacrity he obeys him!

His whole soul is wrapt up in his god! all the powers and faculties of his nature are devoted to his service! and these powers and faculties are ennobled by the intercourse.

Divines tell us that it just ought to be so with Christians—but the dog puts the Christian to shame.—ROBERT BURNS, Scotland's beloved poet.

A Sheath of 'Shaggy Dog' Stories

THE DOG THAT WOULDN'T SPEAK FOREVER AFTERWARD

A man and his dog entered a saloon one day. The man was very thirsty, but as so often happens, did not have the price of a cool glass of beer in his pocket. The man sat down at the bar and his dog leaped up on the stool beside him.

"That's a nice dog you have there," the bartender said. "Perhaps you will trade him for a drink."

"Oh no," said the owner of the dog. "I could not think of that. This is a talking dog."

"I do not believe it," remarked the bartender—"Have him say something."

So the dog spoke up with wide open mouth—"Well, bartender, I'll have a dark beer with pretzels."

The bartender was amazed. "Are those the only words you taught him or can he say anything else? Can I ask him any questions?" The man nodded, so the bartender asked—"What is your name?" and "How old are you?"

The dog looked at the bartender and answered—'My name is Prince. I am three years old."

"Wonderful!" exclaimed the bartender. "I will give you $500 for him."

"Well, I really don't want to sell him but it's a deal." So the bartender paid the man $500 while Prince sat dejectedly on the stool. As the man walked out the door he looked back. The dog was speaking to the bartender:

"That was a very cruel act of my master. I am heart-sick. Just for that, I'll never say another word as long as I live."

PS—The dog's owner was a ventriloquist.

THE BIDDING DOG

At the auction a dog was being offered for sale. The price ran rather high. Finally the successful bidder said to the auctioneer—"That's a pretty high price for this dog. I hope he's worth it."

"Well," said the auctioneer "You have a dog than can talk." "That so? How do you figure that out?" The auctioneer replied: "Who do you think has been bidding against you all this time?"

TWO OLIVES IN A MARTINI

It was a quiet day in the tavern with the usual elbow-benders at the bar. Suddenly the swinging doors opened and an enormous shaggy dog entered the tavern. He walked to the bar, sat up on a chair and pounding the bar with his paws said to the bartender: "Give me a Martini." The bartender said "Okay" and as he turned to mix the drink, the shaggy dog added "And put two olives in the Martini."

The bartender served the drink; the dog drank it with relish, wiped his mouth with his paw, got off the chair and walked out.

The men at the bar shook their heads and were utterly amazed. "Never saw or heard anything like this," muttered one of them to the bartender, who replied: "Oh, that's nothing—a lot of customers like two olives in their Martinis."

A SAINTLY, SHAGGY DOG STORY

The theatrical booking agent was meditating at his desk when the telephone rang. "Would you have a place for a good juggler?" the voice asked at the other end of the phone.

"No, no—not at all," replied the booking agent irritably. "Those juggling acts are a dime a dozen."

"Well," continued the voice "Could you use a good ventriloquist act?" "No" shouted the agent, "They too are passe."

A further word from the voice: "Well, if the ventriloquist would also recite some of his poetry as part of the act, would that make any difference?"

"Please!" remonstrated the agent, "My time is valuable. I cannot listen to any more requests."

"But" said the voice at the other end, "I do juggling and am a ventriloquist, and I write poetry, but would it make any difference to you if I tell you I am a Saint Bernard?"

THE POINTER SUPREME

Down South the bird dog is a prized animal. Two Tennesseans were arguing the relative merits of their pointers. "Now take my dog Prince," said one of them. "I was out hunting one day and couldn't locate my dog. He should have pointed a covey of quail by this time. I searched for him and saw him stopping before a sign which he was looking at intently. I was just about to punish him for loitering when I noticed the sign read: "No dogs allowed on these premises."

The listening Tennessean was equal to the occasion. "That's good," he remarked "but my Sport really is the best bird dog in the state. Just the other day in Memphis we were walking thru the city park when suddenly Sport got on point directly in front of a man sitting on a park bench."

"I looked around everywhere but couldn't see any game or where any birds might be hiding. I conveyed my confusion to the man sitting on the bench. We got into conversation and Sport was still on point. The stranger introduced himself to me saying: "My name is Partridge."

TO BLANCO

My dear, dumb friend, low-lying there,
  A willing vassal at my feet,
Glad partner of my home and fare,
  My shadow in the street,

I look into your great, brown eyes,
  Where love and loyal homage shine,
And wonder where the difference lies
  Between your soul and mine.

For all of good that I have found
  Within myself, or human kind,
Hath royally informed and crowned
  Your gentle heart and mind.

I scan the whole broad earth around
  For that one heart which, real and true,
Bears friendship without end or bound,
And find the prize in you.

I trust you as I trust the stars;
  Nor cruel loss, nor scoff, nor pride,
Nor beggary, nor dungeon bars,
  Can move you from my side.

Ch. ROMANY ROUGH WEATHER.
BY ROMANY RELIANCE EX MARLE HILL MINIVER (OWNED BY MISS WILLIAMS PARTNER OF MISS MONTAGUE-JOHNSON.)

A DOG AND A MAN

He was a dog
But he stayed at home
And guarded the family night and day.

He was a dog
That didn't roam.
He lay on the porch or chased the stray—
The tramps, the burglar, the hen, away;
For a dog's true heart for that household beat
At morning and evening, in cold and heat.
He was a dog.

He was a man,
And didn't stay
To cherish his wife and his children fair.

He was a man.
And every day
His heart grew callous, its love-beats rare,
He thought of himself at the close of day.
And, cigar in his fingers, hurried away
To the club, the lodge, the store, the show.
But—he had a right to go, you know.
He was a man.

—ANONYMOUS

PARTING FROM TRUE FRIENDS

When Sir Walter Scott, the great novelist, was threatened with the loss of his Abbotsford estate he wrote, in part, in his diary, on December 18, 1825:

How live a poor indebted man when I was once the wealthy, the honored? My children are provided; thank God for that. I was to have gone there on Saturday in joy and prosperity to receive my friends. My dogs will wait for me in vain. It is foolish—but the thoughts of parting from these dumb creatures have moved me more than any of the painful reflections I have put down.

Poor things, I must get them kind masters; there may be yet those who loving me may love my dog because it has been mine. I must end this, or I shall lose the tone of mind with which men should meet distress.

I find my dogs' feet on my knees. I hear them whining and seeking me everywhere—this is nonsene, but it is what they would do, could they know how things are.

(The following excerpt from Scott's Writings is often quoted.)

The Almighty who gave the dog to be companion of our pleasure and our toils hath invested him with a nature noble and incapable of deceit. He forgets neither friend nor foe, remembers with accuracy both benefit and injury. He hath a share of man's intelligence but no share of man's falsehood. You may bribe an assassin to slay or a witness to take his life by false accusation, but you cannot make a dog tear his benefactor. He is the friend of man save when man justly incurs his enmity.

SCOTTISH NOVELIST ON DOGS

The Almighty who gave the dog to be the companion of our pleasures and our trials, hath invested him with a nature noble and incapable of deceit. He forgets neither friend nor foe, remembers with accuracy both benefit and injury, and hath a share of man's intelligence but no share of man's falsehood.—SIR WALTER SCOTT.

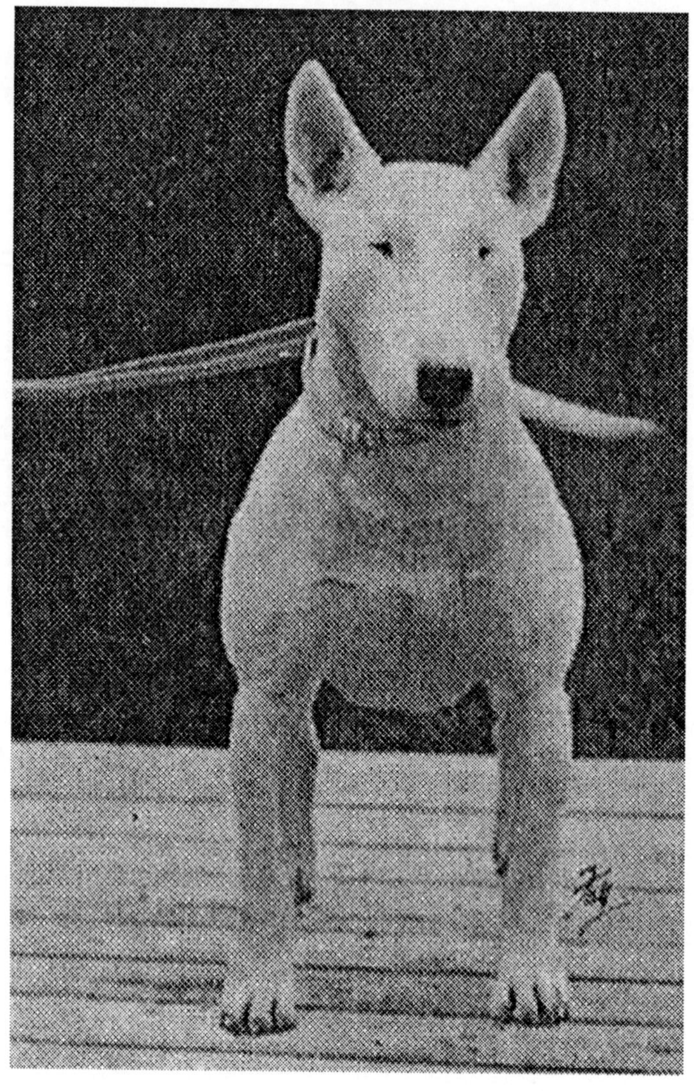

Ch. ORMANDY'S MR. MCGUFFIN.

(OWNED AND BRED BY RAYMOND OPPENHEIMER.)

ARGUS

When wise Ulysses, from his native coast
Long kept by wars, and long by tempests tost,
Arrived at last—poor, old, despised, alone,
To all his friends, and e'en his queen, unknown,
Changed as he was, with age, and toils, and cares,
Furrowed his rev'rend face, and white his hairs,
In his own palace forced to ask his bread,
Scorned by those slaves his former bounty fed,
Forgot of all his own domestic crew,
His faithful dog his rightful master knew!
Unfed, unhoused, neglected, on the clay
Like an old servant, now cashiered, he lay;
And though ev'n then expiring on the plain,
Touched with resentment of ungrateful man,
And longing to behold his ancient lord again,
Him when he saw, he rose, and crawled to meet
('Twas all he could), and fawned, and kissed his feet,
Siezed with dumb joy; then falling by his side,
Owned his returning lord, looked up, and died.
—ALEXANDER POPE

(This tribute is classic, being based upon the incident in Homer's Odyssey.)

ADVICE TO A DOG

Say truth good dogge, and doe not spare to barke,
But snarle and snappe at every sneaking thief,
Let not a Curre goe leering in the darke,
But shew thy kind, bough like a dogge, be briefe;
Lie at the door, give warning to the house,
Scratch at a flea, but care not for a louse.
—*Nicollo Machiavelli (1469 - 1527)*

DOGGE-GONE FUNNY

Many pretty ridiculous aspersions are cast upon dogges so that it would make a dogge laugh to hear and understand them. As I have heard a many say, I am as hot as a dogge or as cold as a dogge. I sweat like a dogge (when indeed a dogge never sweats); as drunke as a dogge; he swore like a dogge and one told a man once that his wife was not to be believed for shee would lye like a doggee.—From The Worlde Runnes on Wheeles.

PHILOSOPHERS

The dogs are God's philosophers—
Though oft beset by fleas,
Because the masters, whom they love,
Eliminate not these.

Were things reversed, the human folk,
Infected with like 'bores',
Man's world were filled with dissonance,
At pain the dog ignores.

Ye-praters of real consequence,
Ye human folk - 'divine',
Or so you think, forget ye not
To note a doggie's whine.
—Madge Acton Mansfield (Ohio poetess—1958)

Mr. Bruce's Bull Terriers, Sam and Toy, in Camp, in Upper Burma.

QUOTES FROM LITERATURE

SHAKESPEARE ON DOGS

I had rather be a dog and bay the moon.—Shakespeare.

Cry 'havoc' and let slip the dogs of war.—Shakespeare.

You play the spaniel and think with the wagging of your tongue to win me.—Shakespeare.

Like Hercules himself, do what he may,

The cat will mew and dog will have his day.—Shakespeare.

Mastiff, greyhound, mungril grim,
Hound or spaniel, brache or lym,
Or bobtail tike, or trundle tail.
Shakespeare's King Lear—III-6.

My hounds are bred out of the Spartan kind . .
and their heads are hung
With ears that sweep away the morning dew
Shakespeare's Midsummer Night's Dream, 4-1

SOME ITALIAN PROVERBS ON CANE (DOG)

Every dog is lion in his own house.

Cut off a dog's tail and he is still a dog.

Where there are no dogs, the fox is king.

A good dog and a good wife stay at home.

German proverb—he that represents himself as a dog must also bark like a dog.

ST. ROCHE—patron saint of dogs, on his deathbed. (13th century).

A soft caress fell on my cheek,
My hands were thrust apart.
And two big sympathizing eyes
Gazed down into my heart.

And of St. Roche's death:

Exempt from blame, he gave up his soul
As a good Christian, in the arms of his dog.

DOGGY ADVICE IN DOGGEREL

I've led a wild life;
  I've earned what I've spent;
I've paid all I've borrowed;
  I've lost all I've lent,
I loved a woman—
  That came to an end;
Get a good dog, boys,
  He'll be your real friend.

—ANONYMOUS (if it ever had an author).

DOGGEREL

A man may smile and bid you hail,
  Yet wish you to the devil;
But when a good dog wags his tail,
  You know he's on the level.

—*ANONYMOUS* (an author who has written many things about dogs).

MRS. BROWNING'S FLUSH

Flush the cocker spaniel owned by the English poetess Elizabeth Barrett Browning has been immortalized in story and stage play. She wrote of him during the last years she spent in the sick chamber:

And if one or two quick tears
dropped upon his glossy ears,
Or a sigh came double—
Up he sprang in eager haste
Fawning, fondling, breathing fast,
In a tender trouble.

AUTHOR'S NOTE—any 'initiated' dog owner confirms this reaction for hasn't his own dog, when a sigh or sound of pain or quick exclamation, escaped one's lips, tho seemingly sleeping, get up, look anxiously and come to your side to inquire whether everything was all right.

TRIBUTE TO A SPANISH BREED

The great pyrenees is a huge-sized dog, now fully recognised in dog shows thruout the world, yet seldom receives the praises due him. Here is an excerpt from the Shepherd Dog of the Pyrenees, written by ELLEN MURRAY.

When day at last
Broke, and the gray fog lifted, there I saw
On that ledge, against the dawning light,
My little one asleep, sitting so near
That edge that as I looked his red barette
Fell from his nodding head down the abyss.
And there, behind him, crouched Pierrot; his teeth,
His good, strong teeth, clenching the jacket brown,
Holding the child in safety. With wild bounds
Swift as the gray wolf's own I climbed the steep,
And as I reached them Pierrot beat his tail,
And looked at me, so utterly distressed.
With eyes that said: 'Forgive, I could not speak,'
But never loosed his hold till my dear rogue
Was safe within my arms.

DOG BECOMES 'FIRST FRIEND'

And the woman said: 'His name is not Wild Dog any more, but the First Friend, because he will be our friend for always and always and always.' —From one of Rudyard Kipling's stories.

Mr. C. Bruce's SAM and YOUNG SAM.
YOUNG SAM (in the foreground) is a son of SAM and TOY, and was bred in Burma.

A PROMINENT SPORTSMAN.
Sir Harry Preston, a great lover of dogs, always had a special liking for the Bull Terrier and has here posed for his photograph with his favourite dog.

Printed in the United Kingdom
by Lightning Source UK Ltd.
120872UK00001B/262-264